THE GLORIES OF MAGADHA

THE GLORIES OF MAGADHA

By

J. N. Samaddar

With a Foreword by

A. B. Keith

The Glories of Magadha

ISBN : 978-81-212-0044-8

First Published 1986, reprint 2014 in India by
Gyan Publishing House
23, Main Ansari Road, Daryaganj,
New Delhi - 110002
Phones : 23282060, 23261060
Fax : (011) 23285914
E-mail: books@gyanbooks.com
website: gyanbooks.com

Printed at : Sagar Color Scan, New Delhi.

SIR HENRY WHEELER K. C. S. I., K. C. I. E.

To

Sir Henry Wheeler

K.C.S.I., K.C.I.E., I.C.S. (Retd.)

During whose chancellorship of the Patna University these Readership Lectures were delivered and who as Chancellor kindly accepted the dedication of the first edition and to whom, by permission, this second edition is also dedicated, as a humble token of all that he has done for the advancement of the Education of the Province of my adoption.

NOTE TO THE FIRST EDITION

My first words are those of deepest thanks to His Excellency the Hon'ble Sir Henry Wheeler for having so kindly accepted the dedication of my Lectures. I owe a debt to His Excellency which it is not easy to acknowledge in terms which shall be adequate to my own sense of obligation and not repugnant to him. I am no less grateful to the Hon'ble Sir Muhammad Fakhruddin, our Ministei of Education, for having not only proposed me for the Readership but also for having opened the course of Lectures ; to Mr. S. Sultan Ahmad, our Vice-Chancellor for having closed the course ; to Mr. V. H. Jackson, M.A., I.E.S., our ex-Vice-chancellor, and to Mr. G. E. Fawcus. M.A., I.E.S., O.B.E., our Director of Public Instruction, for encouragement in various ways.

To Dr. A. B. Keith I am very grateful for the Foreword as well as for various useful suggestions. Likewise I have to thank Drs. Jolly and Poussin for going through the manuscripts and suggesting improvements. Mr. J. A. Chapman, Librarian of the Imperial Library, and Babu Mohendranath Auddy, of the same Library, Calcutta, have every now and then found out references for me. The Index has been prepared by Mr. Santosh Kumar Ghosh, B. A., of the Post Graduate Department of our College, who has also materially helped me in seeing theo ok through the Press. I owe them my heartfelt thanks.

Owing to want of some diacritical marks, some unfortunate mistakes of printing have crept in, but as they do not vitiate the meaning of the passages where they occur, I have not thought it necessary to put in a correction note.

With reference to the many imperfections, (anu I am fully conscious of them), I can only repeat the words of Hemachandra : May the noble-minded scholars instead of cherishing ill-feelings, kindly correct whatever errors may have been committed here, through the dullness of my intellect, in the way of wrong interpretations and mis-statements."

PATNA COLLEGE,
PATNA,
December, 1924.

J. N. S.

NOTE TO THE SECOND EDITION

The intention of the author was to see the second edition carefully through the Press, but unfortunately he was ill throughout the period and seeing the book through, was left entirely to his son, 2nd Lieut. M. L. Samaddar (P. U. T. C.), B. A., of the Patna College. He hereby expresses his indebtedness to friends who favoured him with constructive criticisms and as he, by no means, claims to have said the last word on any question, he does not think it necessary to reply to the one or two adverse criticisms. He would repeat a second time, the pregnant words of Hemachandra, referred to in his Note to the Frist Edition.

The Index, this time, has been prepared by Master Sourendra Nath Samaddar who has also helped in the passing of the Proofs.

PATNA COLLEGE,
PATNA,
August, 1927.

J. N. S.

THE GLORIES OF MAGADHA

CONTENTS

LECTURE I

LECTURE II

The Capitals Of Magadha 39-66

LECTURES III & IV

The Edicts Of Asoka 71-117

LECTURE V

THE UNIVERSITY OF NĀLANDĀ 119-144

LECTURE VI

THE UNIVERSITY OF VIKRAMAŚILĀ 145-172

FOREWORD

The revival of Indian national life has, almost inevitably, been accompanied by the growth of historical interest in the past achievements and glories of Bhāratavarsa. It was the great merit of the late Mr. Vincent Smith to indicate the many fascinating historical problems that must be solved before it became possible accurately to delineate as a whole the vicissitudes of Indian civilisation, and he was fortunate enough to live to see the rising of a school of young Indian Scholars, equipped with the skill and assiduity necessary for the unravelling of the tangled skein of the development of Indian polity. The immediate need is the preparation of monographs on diverse aspects of the subject, to serve as the foundation of a comprehensive and authoritative picture of Hindu Government.

The author of this very interesting treatise on the Glories of Magadha has already established his capacity for useful work by his valuable monograph on the economic condition of ancient India, and not only the general reader but also the expert will find matter for profitable study in his examination of the history of the Magadhan Capitals, of the edicts of Asoka, and of the fate of the monasteries of Nālandā and Vikramaśilā. Much has already been written on these topics, but even more remains to be done to clear up obscurities and elicit the facts, and despite divergence of view on not a few points, I have much confidence in commending these lectures as an earnest and able contribution to an important field of study.

The University of Edinburgh,
28th April, 1924,

A. Berriedale Keith.

The Hon'ble Sir Syed Md. Fakhruddin, Minister of Education, Bihar and Orissa, in introducing the University Reader, observed:—

"GENTLEMEN,

"We have met here this evening to hear the first of the series of interesting lectures to be delivered by Prof. J. N. Samaddar on "The Glories of Magadha". Prof. Samaddar, our University Reader, requires no introduction whatever to you. He has been with us for over a decade and during this period he has proved himself a keen scholar of Archæology and Economics and a successful Professor with his students invariably obtaining maximum marks in his subject at the highest examination of our University. As a Professor he has also been deservedly popular, sympathetic towards his students and able to kindle in them high aspirations.

Year before last he was invited by the University of Calcutta to deliver a course of lectures on the economic condition of Ancient India. These lectures, which have been published by that University, have been very well received throughout the world. I have read these lectures and also the remarks made by great scholars and scientists of England, France, Germany, Italy and America, and every one of them has highly spoken of his work. For a maiden work and a new-comer, this must have been very gratifying to him as it has been to us, his friends, and I take this opportunity to congratulate him publicly, which I have already done in private, for his erudite work.

Following the Calcutta University, His excellency the Chancellor, on the recommendation of the Senate of our University, appointed him a Reader and I am glad to inform you that it was I who had first suggested his name for the Readership. Owing to the financial condition of our University it was not possible to pay him the remuneration as a Reader; but Prof. Samaddar rose to the occasion and agreed to serve without remuneration. I shall be glad if he secures another Readership which may be remunerative.

I have glanced through the learned course of lectures which he is going to deliver on "The Glories of Magadha" and I can bear testimony to the high standard of these lectures. Myself a man of Magadha, I cannot but feel that he has laid us under an obligation by laying before us the glories of our dear Province and I am sure it will give an impetus to all to improve its condition, so that it may again rise to the high position it at one time attained.

I now call upon Prof. Samaddar to commence his lectures."

The Didarganj Image.

(As it was first found by the author of this book)

Frontispiece.

THE GLORIES OF MAGADHA

LECTURE I

The land we live in

The land we live in, with its two ancient capitals of Girivraja and Pāṭaliputra, has a history which is undoubtedly unique, at any rate, unrivalled, not only in India, but perhaps, in the whole world. From whatever point of view we study it, it has something to be proud of. In the domain of spirituality, it was the centre of the activities of religious leaders like Vardhamāna Mahāvīra and Gautama Buddha[1]. The former, related to the royal family of Magadha[2], spent a considerable portion of his life here, while the all-important moment in the career of the Tathāgata, when the supreme knowledge of enlightenment came to that Great Being by virtue of which he attained actual Buddhahood which made him one of the saviours of the world, occurred in Magadha[3]. This alone would invest the land we live in with unprecedented sanctity, not only in the eyes of those vast millions who follow his teachings even now but also of others. The Jains held a great council at Pāṭaliputra, and the two first Buddhist

Importance of Magadha

---

1. Two of the Tīrthankaras can be claimed by this land, the twentieth Subrata, being born at Rājgir, while Mahāvīra, the greatest of the Tīrthaṅkaras, though born at Vaisālī, died in Magadha. Sthūlabhadra was also born in Magadha. *J. B. & O. R. S., V.* 26.

2. Mahāvīra was a near relative of Bimbisāra's queen, the mother of Ajātaśatru. He died at Pāvā in the district of Patna.

3. It may be worth mentioning here that Guru Govinda, the Sikh leader, was born at Pāṭāliputra and his cradle can still be seen at the Sikh temple in this city.

councils[1] were held in Magadha[2]. while the two great[3] teachers amongst the Buddhists, next to Buddha himself, Tissa Moggaliputta and Upagupta, flourished here. The canons of Buddhism were fixed and laid

Aśvaghoṣa

down here, while Aśvaghoṣa, the inspirer of Northern Buddhism known as Mahāyānism,—that Aśvaghoṣa who "stands at the starting point of all the great currents that renewed and transformed India. towards the beginning of the christian era," "poet, musician, preacher, moralist, philosopher, play-wright,"[4] hailed from Magadha[5]. Although this land had been placed under a ban by Brāhmaṇas, it was here that the first historical horse-sacrifice was revived and celebrated with appropriate magnificence, testifying to the revival of Brāhmanical supremacy[6]. The first economist of India, if not of the world, Kauṭilya or Chāṇakya,[7] named

Chāṇakya

also Viṣṇugupta, was, perhaps, born in this land, and certainly had his school and disciples here, while Kāmaṇḍaka, who followed in the footsteps of the

---

1. *The Cambridge History of India*, Vol. 1, p. 165.

2. See *Indian Antiquary*, 1908, article by Prof. L. De La Valle Poussin.

3. *Ibid*, 1, p. 498.

4. Kaniṣka took away from Pāṭaliputra Aśvaghoṣa who presided at the third Buddhist council held under the auspices of that great king. *The Early History of India*, p. 276.

5. "He is an inventor in all these arts and excels in all; in his richness and variety he recalls Milton, Goethe, Kant and Voltaire". Dr. Levi in *Ancient India.*

6. *The Early History of India*, p. 200.

7. For the name, see the *Indian Historical Quarterly*, Vol. I. Dr. A B. Keith is against this. In an article in the *Sir Asutosh Memorial Volume*, he observes: "The proposal to read the author's name as Kauṭalya seems unnecessary. It rests on too recent evidence to claim respect on the score, and the lexicographical authority is late. It is most natural to suppose that, at sometimes or other, it was thought uusuitable to allow the derivation of Kauṭilya from Kuṭila and the form Kauṭilya was devised in lieu with an appropriate Kuṭala as its source. The evidence of early references to the Kauṭilya including those in the Jain texts is clearly decisive in favor of the spelling with I."

father of Economics, can also be claimed by us. That the Science of Economics, with which is associated the Science of Politics, was systematically studied here is on record, while the *Māhabhārata* testifies to the fact that the ministers of Magadha were learned in the Science of Statecraft[1]. Here Upavarṣa and Varṣa, Pánini and Piṅgala[2], Vararuchi and Patañjali[3], rose to eminence. And, if tradition is to be relied on, Kālidāsa was also a native of Magadha[4]. It was in this land that Āryabhaṭṭa[5], the father of scientific Astronomy, was born, while it was the home of Ṛṣis like Chyavaṇa and Dadhīchī. Long before the historical days of Chandragupta Maurya, Magadha could boast of powerful monarchs like Bṛhadratha[6], described as handsome, mighty, immensely rich, and matchlessly powerful having an army of three *Akṣauhiṇis*. Jarāsandha, whom no contemporary king was able to equal in prowess[7], "blazing forth above the heads of all those that wore a crown", is admitted by even the panegyrists of his enemies as having robbed all other kings of their splendour, and whom a host of kings followed[8].

And others

1. *Mahābhārata*, Sabhā, XIX.

2. Piṅgala was the *Guru* of the sons of Bindusāra and specially of Aśoka.

3. There are so many references in Patañjali to Pāṭaliputra that one cannot but conclude that a portion, if not the whole, of his *Mahābhāṣya* was written at the Capital. Cf. Chapter I. 15; III. 2-123.

4. *Indian Antiquary*, 1908, p. 236. The description by Kālidāsa of the king of Magadha in *Raghuvaṃśa*, Canto IV, 21-24 is remarkable.

5. Born in 476.

6. *Mahābhārata*, Sabhā, XVII. Cf. also *Harivaṃśa* cxvii, 659. The eldest Bṛhadratha founded a famous dynasty in Madadha. Twenty-two kings of the line are said to have ruled one after another.

7. *Mahābhārata*, Sabha, XIX. "All the kings remain obedient to him, as all embodied beings remain obedient to the wind." Cf. also Sabhā XIV, XX and XXII.

8. *Harivaṃśa*. Chap. xcviii.

First paramount sovereignty

At the time of the invasion[1] of the Macedonian hero, here was a king whose very name and fame, frightened the unconquerable soldiers of Alexander the great,[2] while the people of the country were considered as the distinguished in all India[3]. The nucleus of the first empire in Northern India was formed by the Saiśunākas here[4]; and it was Magadha and Magadha alone which could claim sovereignty from Afganisthan across the Continent eastward to Bengal, and from the Himalayas to the Central Provinces, while the two great emperors of Northern India, Asoka and Samudra Gupta, sent their victorious banners from Magadha—one to preach to the then civilised world his evangelic mission of Love and *Dhamma*, the other to conquer far-off lands and capitals. And long after, when people were forgetting the glories of Magadha, a king of Magadha, Dharmapāla, again stretched his proud arms to conquer Northern India[5]. From Magadha went out missionaries as evangelists[6] of the highest repute, medical men for the treatment of human beings as well as of lower animals, and for the establishment of hospitals; while it was at the capital of Magadha that vivisection was first experimented upon for the cure of incurable diseases[7].

---

1. I believe here was the first attempt to establish a paramount sovereignty in Northern India. It failed, however, to succeed. Dr. Keith accepts this view of mine.

2. McCrindle. *Alexander's Invasion.* The Magadhan King had the reputation of having an army of 2,00,000 foot, 80,000, cavalry, 8,000 war-chariots and 6000 elephants.

3. McCrindle, *Megasthenes*, p. 66.

4. Śiśunāka is the proper reading. *Vide*, Pargiter, *Journal of the Royal Asiatic Society*, 1915, p. 146.

5. *Epigraphia Indica, IV*, 243.

6. Madhyantika was sent to Kāśmīr and Gandhāra; Mahārakṣita was sent to the *Yavana* or Greek country; Mahādeva Rakṣita, Dharmarakṣita and Mahādarmarakṣita were sent to southern India, Majjhima proceeded to the Himalayas, while Sona and Uttara went to Subarnabhumi.

7. *J. B. & O. R. S.*, V. 28.

Nālanda and Vikramasīlā

The two very old and widely celebrated residential universities of India, perhaps of the world, had their seats in Magadha—Nālandā belonging to the age of artistic culture and skill, boasting "of a gorgeous and luxurious style of architecture, of a deep philosophical knowledge", of profound and learned discussions and of rapid progress along the paths of civilisation[1], and both showing a standard of culture and education which may be emulated by many modern universities. From both[2], teachers went forth to the north and to the east to inculcate knowledge, and to both flocked students from all parts of Asia to imbibe the highest teachings of Religion and Philosophy. It was here that the skill of the stone-cutter attained perfection and he produced models which, as admitted by the learned author of the *Early History of India*[3], would be found to be beyond the craftsmanship of the twentieth century. The engineers and architects of the royal house of Magadha could design and construct spacious and lofty edifices, throw massive embankments, equipped with convenient sluices[4] and other appliances of extraordinary engineering skill, handle enormous monoliths,[5] and polish them in a way which is still unsurpassed, excavate commodious chambers with varnished interiors which, even to-day, would dazzle the eyes of all and build palaces which led people to believe that those must have been built only by superhuman beings and could not have been up reared by human hands[6]. Not only in and around Magadha, but even in distant lands, skilled artists from

1 Broadley, *The Buddhistic Remains of Bihar*, *J. A. S. B.*, 1872.

2. Beal *Buddhist Records of the Western World*, II. 170. Both in points of endowments and efficiency, Nālanda can be emulated by many a modern university. *Vide* Lecture V.

3. *Aśoka*, p. 136.

4. *Megasthenes.*

5. It took a considerable time and expense to uplift a Maurya pillar in Muzaffarpore.

6. *Fo-Kwo-ki.*

Magadha were engaged by kings[1], showing the acme of supremacy the artists had attained in this old land. The Magdhan measure was ordered to be used by the great lawgiver, Manu[2]. It was Magadha which possessed a Government which was better organised than the Government of Akbar or Shah Jahan[3]. Magadha had a civilization and culture in its palmy days, equal, if not superior, to that which India attained, eighteen or nineteen hundred years later. This fact has been admitted by historians, and Magadha need not fear any comparison in point of historical interest with any part of India.

Condemnation of Magadha

Such was Magadha, which was the most famous kingdom in ancient India, and three-fourths of India's early history is the history of Magadha. But this great land, of which we are speaking in strains of unbounded enthusiasm and praise,was regarded with deadly aversion by the Vedic Aryans. The thirtieth Book of the *Vājasaneyi saṃhitā*[4] enumerating the victims of the *Puruṣamedha*, makes the god Savitā bound to the sacrificial stake a Māgadha to be dedicated as sacrifice to the deity of excessive noise[5], In the *Pañchaviṃśa*

---

1. Cf *Rāmāyaṇa*, XI., 23. Also *The Tamils—1800 years ago*. As late as the 8th or 9th century A. D. a temple-builder had to be taken from Magadha for the Central Provinces. *Epigraphia Indica*, XI. 188. The Silimpur inscription was inscribed by a Magadhan artist. *Ibid.* Vol. xiii.

2. The weights and measures to be used by the physician are expressly enjoined to be those of Magadha.

3. V. A. Smith, *Aśoka*, p. 238.

4. XXX. 5,22.

5 Weber with reference to this asks, "What is to be understood by *atikrushta* ? If we take *atikrushta* in the sense of "great noise", the most obvious interpretation of Māgadha is to understand it with Medatithi in its epic sense as signifying ministrel, son of a Vaiśya by a Kṣatriya." Quoting Sāyana, Weber says, "Sāyana commenting on the corresponding passage of the *Taitt. Brāhmaṇa* iii. 4. 1. explains the word *atikrushta* by *atininditādevaya*, dedicated to the very blameworthy as his deity." Mr. Pargiter also in his latest book, *Ancient Indian Historical Tradition*, p. 16, refers to the Māgadha as a bard and speaking of the

Brāhmaṇa[1] we are told that they were distinct in culture from the Aryans, while in *Srauta Sūtra* there is also a condemnation of them[2]. In the *Aitareya Āraṇyaka* the people of Magadha are treated as bards[3], and again, in the *Sāṃkhayana Āraṇyaka* it was unusual for a Brahāmaṇa to dwell in the territory of Magadha. With none of the one hundred and thirty-three Asvamedhas instituted by Bharata, son of Dusmanta, is associated Magadha.

Indeed, all the earlier and later Vedie texts displayed a marked antipathy towards the people of Magadha, to whom malarial fever was assigned, evidently as a curse, for the land was seemingly considered[4] as not worth living in as being not within the pale of Vedic civilization. Apparently, the country was not in good repute with the Vedic people, and a Brāhmaṇa living then in the Magadha country was called *Brahmabandhu* —a degraded Brāhmaṇa[5], In the Smṛti literature,

Antipathy to Magadha

fable which says that the first Sūta and Māgadha came into existence at the sacrifice of king Pṛthu, son of Veṇa, concludes that the Māgadhas were really inhabitants of Magadha.

1. XVII. 16. Cf. *J. R. A. S.*, 1913, p. 159.

2. VII. 6. 28. Cf. *Kātyāyana S. S.* XXII. 422.

3. II. 1-1. This passage, however, has been differently interpreted, one class of scholars suggesting an amendment *Vaṅga Māgadha* (*i. e.* Vaṅgas and Māgadhas two neighbouring peoples). Mahāmahopādhyāya H. P. Sastri observes, "for between Baṅga and Chera or the Dravidian people in Chotanagpore, the whole country had a tribe called Bāgdis."

4. *Atharva*, V. 22, 14. Commenting on this, Roth in his *Literature and History of the Vedas*, observes: "The Aṅgas and Māgadhas are tribes in South Bihar and the country bordering it on the west. We have thus in this verse two nations situated on the north-west and two to the south-east, whom we may suppose, from the maledictions pronounced on them, to have been hostile or alien tribes, who lived on the borders of Brāhmanic idea and to have been beyond its boundaries at the time when this incantation was composed" We shall refer to it later on.

5 In one passage only, however, the Brāhmaṇa *Madhyama pratibodhiputra* who lived in Magadha was considered as a very respectable Brāhmaṇa. (*K. Āraṇyaka*, viii, 13), though Oldenberg in his *Buddha*, p. 400, regarded this as unusual—a view accepted by Macdonell and Keith in *Vedic Index*, II. 116.

Magadha was included in the list of countries migration to which was strictly forbidden and a penance was necessary for having gone there[1]. This dislike continued even to the days of Manu, where Magadha is not included by the lawgiver in the list of the Brahmarṣi lands. Even as late as in the *Bhabisya Brahma-Khaṇḍa*, it is mentioned that the people of Magadha would be destitute of good manners. And you will be surprised to hear that the land of Magadha even now, is under a ban, for Brāhmaṇas of Mithilā will avoid bathing on this side of the Ganges on auspicious occasions.

Present dislike

It may be mentioned that the name Magadha[2] is

1. *Baudhāyana Dharmasūtra* I, 12.

2. "Magadha corresponds, at least in the time of the Buddha to the modern District of Gayā. The inhabitants of this region still call it Magā, a name doubtless derived from Magadha."—Sir George Grierson in *E. R. E. V.* 181. The boundaries were probably the Ganges to the north, the Sone to the west, a dense forest reaching to the plateau of Chota Nagpur to the south and Aṅga to the east". *The Cambridge History of India*, Vol. I, p. 182. In the map of India, which illustrates Mr. Talboy Wheeler's *History* of these remote times, the territories of Magadha are shewn to the south of the river Ganges, bounded on one side by Mithilā and on the other by Baṅga, or Bengal At the time of Buddha it contained 80,000 villages (*Vinaya*, I. 179) and was 300 leagues in circumferrence. I. 148. The *Mahāvagga* speaks of Magadha as possessing 80,000 townships, while the king had an assembly of 10,000 overseers over these townships. *S. B. E.*, XVII, I. In the Bhabrā Edict, Aśoka is styled as the king of Magadha. "The word Bihar has in turn served to designate several artificial divisions. The name originally belonged to the ancient city, which from its far-famed seat of Buddhistic learning was distinguished by the name of Vihār. The Muhammadan conquerors of the city extended its name to the surrounding country, of which it became the capital ; and at the time of Akbar it came to signify that important portion of eastern India comprised in the seven Sirkars of Mungar, Champaran, Hajipur, Saran, Tirhut, Rohtas and Bihar. This was Subah Bihar. Under British rule, Subah Bihar and Subah Bengal were united under a joint government, while the Zila surrounding the capital and which bore its name, was divided into Zila Patna and Zila Gaya." *The Buddhistic Remains o, Bihar* by A. M. Broadley, but *vide* also *The Cambridge History of India* Vol. I. p. 57, where in Bihar has been included both Videha and Magadha. "The Māgadhas who inhabited the Patna and Gaya districts of S. Bihar are well-known by their name to the *Rigveda* ; but together with their neighbours, the Aṅgas, in the districts of Monghyr and Bhāgalpur, they are mentioned in the *Atharvaveda*". *The Cambridge History of India*, Vol. I, p. 309.

not actually referred to in the Ṛgveda. The word *Kīkaṭa* occurs only in one passage in the Ṛgveda where it appears as hostile to the singer. The only thing which the Ṛgveda mentions about the *Kīkaṭas* is their kine, which the hymnist regretfully mentions as being of no use in sacrifice, though he covets them to use their milk for sacrificial purposes[1]. The term *Kīkaṭa* has been used as a synonym for Magadha ; and, hence, it has been concluded that the *Kīkaṭas* were a non-Aryan people living in the country now known as Magadha.

It may be observed, in passing, that various European scholars have come to different conclusions regarding the interpretation of this word. E. G. Zimmer asserted that the *Kīkaṭas* were a non-Aryan people living in the land latterly known as Magadha. Weber held that these people were Aryans, though at variance with the other Aryan tribes[2]. Indian commentators also have different views. Yāṣka in his *Nirukta* refers to the *Kīkaṭas* as living in non-Aryan land. The author of the *Vāyu Purāṇa*[3] identified *Kīkaṭa* with Magadha, while the commentator S'ṛīdhara indentified it with *Gayā Pradeśa*. Kīkata

Closely connected with this question and the early history of Magadha, is the mention of the term Vrātya and his occupation and position, for in many ways, he was connected with Magadha. The name Magadha is brought into a significant connexion with the *Vrātya* in a mystic hymn, which has even now, after centuries, not been clearly explained. In the fifteenth book of the *Atharvaveda* in the so-called *Vrātya* book the *Vrātya*[4] Vrātya

1 Griffith explaining this passage observes, "the cows bestowed by Indrā are unprofitable when in the possession of those who do not worship the Aryan Gods".

2 *Indian Literature.* Weber's reasoning that because Magadha was later a seat of Buddhism and hence was held in bad repute cannot hold good, for long before the introduction of Buddhism it was in that state.

3 Vide *The Rājagṛha Māhātyam.*

4 Charpentier saw in the *Vrātyas,* the precursors of the Sivaites of

is brought into special relation with the *puṃschali* and *māgadhi* faith, is called his harlot, the *mitra* (friend) his Māgadha ; and similary, the dawn, the earth (?), the lighting, his harlots, *hāsa* (scorn), the thunder, his Māgadham. "A more connected account of the *Vrātyas* is found in the *Pan'chavimsa Brāhmaṇa* of the Sāmaveda and the Sūtras of that Veda. It is clear that, as their name suggests, they were persons regarded as outcasts ; and ceremonies are described intended to secure them admission into the Brāhmanical fold. The description of the *Vrātyas* well suits nomad tribes : they are declared not to practise agriculture, to go about in rough wagons, to wear turbans, to carry goads and a peculiar kind of bow, while their garments are of a special kind. Their sense of justice was not that of the Brāhmaṇas, and their speech, though it seems Aryan, was apparently Prākritic in form, as is suggested by the significant remark that they called what was easy of utterance but hard to speak"[1]. Owing to the obscurity of the *Vrātya* book, the meaning of these passages, as I have already stated, is not altogether clear. But it is evident that that book of the *Atharvaveda* dealing with the *Vrātyas*—the inexplicable book—glorifies the *Vrātya*, as a type of the supreme power in the universe[2]. That Magadha was recognised as the chief centre of *Vrātya* culture is evident from the fact that in the Srauta Sútras of

---

to-day. But this view has not been accepted. Cf. *J. R. A. S.*, 1913, Dr. Keith's learned article, p. 155.

1 *The Cambridge History of India*, Vol. I, p. 124. The difficulty of the *Vrātyas* to pronounce the vedic speech was evidently due to its conjunct consonants which the Prākrirs avoid. See *Ibid.*, p. 146. Also the annual address of Mahāmahopādhāyaya Haraprasad Śāstri in the Asiatic Society of Bengal, published in the *J. A. S. B.*, 1921.

2. This is considered as an evidence that the *Atharvaveda* which glorifies the *Vrātyas* was composed by the Aryans who had settled in Magadha, the land of the *Vrātyas*. This is also, perhaps, one of the reasons why the *Atharvaveda* is not always accepted as the fourth Veda.

Lāṭyāyana[1] and Kāṭyāyana[2], it is enjoined that after the *Vrātyastoma*, a rite that procured the admission of the *Vrātya* to the Brāhmaṇic fold, his belonging or outfit had to be bestowed either upon an inferior Brāhmaṇa, one in name only[3], of Magadha, or one who had given up the *Vrātya* practices. This evidently proves that the Aryan Brāhmaṇas who had advanced farther and had settled in Magadha were looked down upon, should we say as *Vrātyas* or as priests of the Māgadhas, and consequently the mass of the population of Magadha was also looked down upon. It seems the people and their priests were alike treated with disfavour.

The reason of the condemnation

But why was Magadha looked down upon? Why were her people held in contempt? What was her fault and what was their fault? How and why did the Vedic Aryans condemn this land and her people? Fick[4] has suggested that the low opinion formed of Magadha and of *Magadhadeśīya Brāhmaṇa* might have been due to the low estimate in which the western Brāhmaṇas held Magadha, which was at a great distance from them and which was not Brāhmanized; partly also, that the people of Magadha, their priests or Brāhmaṇas, at any rate, may have acquired this bad reputation. The learned authors of the *Vedic Index* support Oldenberg[5] and lay it down to the fact that the Māgadhas were not really Brāhmanized. This", they say, "is entirely in accord with the evidence of the *Satapatha Brāhmaṇa* that neither Kośala, nor Videha, was fully Brāhmanized, at an early date, much less, Magadha."[6] Referring to Weber's suggestion which might have

1 VIII 6. 28.
2 XXII. 4. 22.
3 *Brahmabandhu*.
4 Calcutta University Edition, pp. 215—216.
5 *Buddha*. 400 n.
6 *Vedic Index*, II. 116.

influenced the question, *viz*, the persistence of aboriginal blood and the growth of Buddhism, it may be rightly pointed out that the latter consideration was hardly applicable to the *Yajurveda* or the ***Atharvaveda***. Oldenberg also thought that Magadha along with some other countries, such as Aṅga, Kāṣi, Kośala and Videha, were the abodes of earlier Aryan immigrants[1], *i.e.*, they were pioneers in advance of the general body of the Aryans, and as such, were looked down upon by their brethern. As Aryans, who were the first to migrate, their actions were not favourably considered, rather these were condemend.

Magadha—an Aryan settlement

Magadha was indeed on the extreme confines of Aryan civilization and culture, where Indo-Aryan influence had not penetrated fully, and dwelling in the Magadha country was considered as something unusual—at any rate, was not approved of. Magadha in the early Vedic times was only a SETTLEMENT of the Aryans, the main horde was still lagging behind, and certainly had not advanced so far. And, even at a later time, when the Kuru-Pañchāla civilisation had established itself, we hear of Magadha being spoken of as a SETTLEMENT. The significance of a passage in the ***Mahābhārata*** in this connexion cannot be overestimated: "O son of Pṛtha thus shines the great beautiful Magadha SETTLEMENT possessed of cattle, ever full of water, free from diseases and rich in good houses." Magadha, indeed, was a SETTLEMENT[2] of the Aryans; it does not matter in which ethnogical

1 *Buddha*. p. 10.

2 *Vide Mahābhārata*, Sabhā. Ch. XXI. V. II, In this connection it is interesting to note the views of a profound scholar like Mr. Pargiter who in the *J. R. A. S.* 1908, p. 852, refers to his article in the *J. A. S. B.*, Vol. LXVI, part I (p 85), and says that "certain tribes belonging to a closely connected ethnic group probably invaded India from the sea, setting first along the west and north-west of the Bay of Bengal, and gradually pushed inwards up the Ganges valley. They occupied a wedge-shaped area, with its base along the sea-coast

wave the Aryans reached this province, but those who came and with them, the land, its inhabitants and settlers all were condemned.

This is not the first time that such a thing had happened in the history of Aryan India. The example of *Paṇis*, who have been characterised as the demons of darkness for their greediness and hoarded wealth, but who were also Aryans having made themselves prominent by their trading and mercantile habits, and who also were condemned, may be cited. In the case of the Aryans advancing leaving their brethren behind, and settling in Magadha, we find a repetition of the same old story.

The people, who had come in advance and had SETTLED in Magadha, were not Non-Aryans, but were pure Aryans whose liberal views, or FORWARDNESS in advancing beyond the country of their brethern, brought on them the hatred of those whom they had left behind in the west. The growth of a new spirit was inevitable amongst some of the Aryans immediately after their settlement in the Punjab, and even afterwards. Some of them had like the *Paṇis* advanced for purposes of trade, or, as Mahāvīra or Buddha did afterwards, some of them left their hearths and homes actuated by the spirit of teachers. These had to leave their homes in the west to drift into the homeless state so common in the east. The *Vrātya* is described as going to the people, becoming the guest of the king as well as of the ordinary people, to be honoured with a becoming reverence everywhere by his host, in his sojouring to all the points of the compass. He had to preach his message and explain it. Herein was the origin of the

---

and Aṅga and its apex touching Magadha and Videha...Their vanguard and the Aryan vanguard met in Magadha and Videha, and each was arrested there. Aryan influence—political, social and religious, spread gradually over those five nations but did so by virtue of its superiority and not by further aggressive migration".

Vrātyas. Herein was the cause of the spread of Aryan culture among other communities living on the borderland of Aryan culture and civilisation. The *Vrātya* was an Aryan, but the fact that he had left his hearth and home, made his brethern and relations assume a contemptuous attitude towards the country of his adoption. And when we read in the *Pañchavimśa Brāhmaṇa* that the converted *Vrātyas* in order to cut off all connection with their past, had to hand over their wealth to their companions who still preferred to live according to the old mode of life, we have no other conclusion left than to say that their brethern in the west were at once satisfied as they—shall we call them the *Liberals*—handed over their gains which they had acquired by their "go-aheadness". Everything was forgotten after the performance of some ceremonies, re-admitting the lost ones into their own fold—the old Brāhmaṇic fold. As it says, when the Devas ascended *Svarga*, some of their brethern wandered on earth as *Vrātyas.* These latter, being afterwards desirous of joining their fortunate brethren, came to the spot whence they had ascended *Svarga*, but owing to their ignorance of (Vedic) hymns, they could not accomplish their object. The Devas sympathising with their less fortunate brethern, asked the *Maruts* to teach them the necessary hymns. The *Vrātya* Devas, having thus learnt the hymn called *Soḍaśa*, written in the metre called *Anuṣṭubh*, ascended subsequently to *Svarga*. This *Svarga* was the old Brahmanic fold. What did it mean really? It significanily shows that the *Vrātyas* were taken back. They were Aryans, they had no fault but what we would call now their "go-aheadness". The Aryan society was even then exclusive, and no one but the Aryans could have been re-allowed into it. But such was the way in which the forwardness of those who advanced was estimated that long long afterwards, they, as well as the land where they lived, bordering on the verge of Aryan civilisation, were held in bad repute, in spite of the great spiritual and intellectual lead of Magadha and of her people in subsequent times[1].

Videgha Māthava

The legend[2] in the *Satapatha Brāhmaṇa* relating to the national hero, Videgha Māthava, has preserved well the memory of Brāhmaṇism as it spread from the west towards the east. The story is not only interesting but useful, as it speaks of Vedic culture, from the west, the banks of the *Sarasvatī*, till the Brāhmaṇas reached the river *Sadānīra* which they did not cross[3].

And the reason ascribed was that *Agni Vaiśvāṇara*, who from the *Sarasvati*, did not cross the river, and, therefore, in earlier ages no Brāhmaṇa went across the *Sadānīra*[4] to the east, for it was bad land, which *Agni Vaiśvānara* had not tasted. Now, however, eastward of the region dwell many Brāhmaṇas ; now is it indeed good land, for now have Brāhmaṇas made it worthy of habitation through offerings. As Oldenberg has significantly observed, "The difference between the ancient Vedic land of culture in the west and in the east, where there was Aryan land, but not yet for a long-time a home of *Vaiśvānara* can scarcely be significantly expressed"[4].

---

1 Mr. A. Chakravarti writing in the *Jain Gazette*, June 1925, on the *Vrātyas* concludes : "The term Vrātya first denoting respect and spiritual purity was applied to the religious protestants among the Aryans who were opposed to the ritualism of Indra-cult and afterwards was extended to the lower orders among the new faith."

2 1-4-1-10. ff.

3 The identification of this river is doubtful Oldenberg says "What river that Sadānīra, named as a boundary, is, cannot, as far as I see, be determined with certainty". Weber identified it with the Gaṇdaki, which in later times formed the boundary between the territories of Videha and Kośala. Against this theory the fact seems to speak, that the *Mahābhārata* on one occassion makes its heroes cross *Gaṇḍakina Ca Mahāśoṇam Sadānīram*. This passage is, of course, not decisive for the knowledge of the true Sadānīra which has been lost to later lexicographers in every instance may have been already wanting to the poets who composed these passages of the *Mahābhārata*".

4 Cf. Oldenberg, *Buddha*, p. 400, Mr. Pargiter in *J. A. S. B.* 1891,

Thus was Mithilā first Aryanised, and thence came forward Vedic culture to Magadha and went still further east, till the whole land fell under the influence of Aryan culture and civilisation. Mithilā was thus Aryanised earlier than Magadha, and that is the reason, as stated by me before, why even now the Brāhmaṇas of Mithilā are averse to bathe along the right banks of the Ganges on sacrificial occasions, a reminiscence of the old story and usage[2].

In the list of the sixteen celebrated monarchs given in the *Mahābhārata*, one of the *Soḍasarājikas* was Bṛhadratha Vīra, whom Pargiter has rightly considered as probably Bṛhadratha of Magadha[3], and whose name we have already mentioned. We know also from the Buddhist *Aṅguttara Nikāya*[4] that there were sixteen states of considerable extent and power known as *Solasa* Mahāyanapada of which Magadha was one. What the territory actually was, is very difficult to ascertain, though as mentioned before[5], in the time of

---

referring to this explains that owing to the unhealthiness of Videha, "no Arya would have ventured within it and the only way in which the Aryans could have colonised it was by filling and burning the forest down wholesale and opening out the soil to the purifying rays of the sun". Mr. Pargiter by *Agni Vaiśvānara* means not the sacrifical fire, but fire in its ordinary popular sense, and therefore suggests that Māthava with his comrades burnt the forest down and began cultivating the land and now the Brhāmaṇas finding the new tract developing into a good tract followed afterwards and soon appropriated the merit to themselves and their sacrifices.

1 Mithilā the Capital of Videha is not mentioned in the Vedic texts, but constantly mentioned in the Jātakas and the Epics. For a description of Mithilā, see *Mahājanaka Jātaka*, Cowell's Edition, Vol. VI. 30.

2 *Vide* ante p. 6 "The traces of Indo-Aryan descent, which have been observed in the higher social grades of Bengal and Orissa, must be due to colonisation at a later date". *The Cambridge History of India*, Vol. I 148.

3 *Ancient Indian Tradition*, p. 39 In the *Vāyu Purāṇa*: *Rājagṛha Māhātyam*, Bṛhadratha has been mentioned as the King of Magadha and the father of Jarāsandha.

4 I. 213; IV, 252, 256, 260. The *Mahāvastu* also refers to it in II. 2.

5 *Vide ante*, p. 8.

the Buddha, it corresponded very likely, with the modern districts of Patna and Gaya. From the Purāṇas of which the historical interest centres in Magadha, though composed much later, we get lists of the kings of Magadha, which long before the writing of the Purāṇas, had become the recognized centre of culture, both religious and political. The long line of kings attributed to Magadha by the Purāṇas consists of a series of no fewer than eight dynastic lists, furnished with a statement of the number of years in each reign and the duration of the dynasty. If all these dynasties could be regarded as successive, and if the length of reigns could be determined with certainty the chronology of Magadha would be a simple matter of calculation[1]. But this is not the case; neither is it possible to deal with all the kings in the course of one lecture.

From these Purāṇic lists, we find the name of the Saiśunāga dynasty called by the Purāṇas as Kṣatriyas, to which some historical reality can be given and of which Siśunāga was the founder[2]. Of course, the first important king was Bimbisāra or S'renika[3] with whom began the greatness and supremacy of Magadha by his conquest of the kingdom of Aṅga. Bimbiśāra streng-

1 Cf, Pargiter, *Ancient Indian Tradition.*

2 *The Cambridge History of India*, Vol. 1, p. 310. "In the Purānic lists, the earliest dynasty which can claim historical reality is that known as the Saiśunāga, from the name of its founder, Siśunāga or Siśunāka". *The Early History of India*, p. 32. According to Mr. Pargiter, *J. R. A. S.* 1915, p. 146, Sisunāka is the usual reading. See also *Journal of the Department of Letters*, IX, 58 where Dr. Raichaudhury discusses this question.

3 *Vide J. B. & O. R. S.*, Vol. 1. p. 67 ff, for an article by Mr. Jayaswal on *The Saiśunāka and Maurya chronology and the date of the Buddha's Nirvāna*". Dr. Keith considers, that "the idea that Bimbisāra was the "military" king is one of Mr. Jayaswal's ingenious but unconvincing guesses, and the same remark applies to his interpretation of Kuṇika". Cf. Also *the Indian Historical Quarterly*, *Seṇiya Bimbiśara.*, by Dr. H. C. Rai Chaudhury who refers to the fact that when "Sreṇya", the lord of the country of the Māgadhas, visited Buddha on the Pāṇdava hill, the latter addressed him as a scion of the *Haryaṅka Kūla*". Mr. Vincent Smith credits Bimbisāra with the

thened his position by his marriages with two princesses, one of the family of the Lichchavis of Vaiśali, other of the royal house of Kośala. The former bore him Ajātaśatru to whom he is said to have surrendered the throne after reigning twenty-eight years. After the murder of Bimbisāra[1] by his son Ajātaśatru or Kuṇika[2] the parricide ascended the throne in 554 B.C., an event which may have happened after the death of Mahāvīra, and a few years before the Nirvāna of the Buddha. Both Mahāvīra and the Buddha preached in Magadha during the reign of Bimbisāra. Ajātaśatru annexed the country to the north of ths Ganges, now known as Tirhut, which the

---

building of New Rājagṛha, "the outer town to the north of the ring of hills encircling the ancient fort". *The Early History of India*, p. 32. The Purāṇas attribute a reign of 28 or 38 years to Bimbisāra, one of 25. 27 or 28 to Ajātaśatru. *Kali Age*, 21. Prof Geiger in his Introduction to *Mahāvaṃsa* sets the chronology as follows:—Bimbisāra's birth 558 B. C. : Accession 543 B. C. ; Death 491 B. C. : Ajātaśatru's accession 491 B. C. : Death 459 B. C. According to Dr. Bhandarkar, *Carmichael Lecture*, 1918, Bimbisāra was a general who carved out a kingdom for himself at the expense of the Vajjis and thereby founded a dynasty. The *Mahāvaṃśa*, however, states that Bimbiśara was anointed king by his own father when he was only 15 years old. The late Mr. N. L. De mentions Bhattiya, as the name of the father, *J. A. S. B.*, 1914, p. 321.

1 The Ceylon chronologists place this event eight years before the Buddha's death, at the time when Bimbisāra, who had come to the throne when he was fifteen, had reigned fifty-two years. *The Cambridge History of India*, Vol. I. 184. Both Māhavīra and Buddha preached in Magadha during the reign of Bimbisāra. The chronology, of course, is bound to be uncertain. The Jains spell the name as Techchaki. *Vide* Jacobi, *S. B. E.*, xxii, 216. See also *Indian Antiquary*, 1903, p. 233.

2. Dr. Barnett placing this about 500 B. C. observes: "This led to war with Kośala, in which he apparently was victorious, with the Lichchavis, whom he defeated, capturing Vaiśāli, and perhaps advancing to the foot of the Himalayas. He built a fortress. Pāṭaliputra, which later became the Capital of Magadha". *Antiquities of India*, 37. "It is very doubtful, whether the Sanskrit Śrenika is really the correct representation of the Śeniya of the Piṭakas. If we take it in its simple meaning, one of the Śreni army, "Seniya Bimbisāra", Bimbisāra the military king, we shall probably be near the original meaning, for *S'reni* signifies an army division" *J. B. & O. R. S*, 1. 84. *Vide*, however, the previous f. n. For an account of Ajātaśatru. *Vide* Rhys Davids, *Buddhist India*, p. 14 and Rockhill's *Life of the Buddha*, pp 90-94. See *J. B. & O. R. S.*, V. 550 ff for an interesting suggestion of Mr. K P. Jayaswal that the Pārkham statue at Mathurā represents Ajātaśatru. *Vide* also *J. B. & O. R. S.*, V. 512 ff for the opinion of the late Dr. V. A. Smith on the same.

Lichchavis then occupied. It has been supposed that the invader carried his victorious arms to their natural limit, *i.e.*, the foot of the Himalayas; and that from this the whole region between the Ganges and the Himalayas became subject more or less directly to the suzerainty of Magadha[1]. At any rate, this was the beginning of the greatness of Magadha, but as this subject is of more than a passing interest, and is rather of a momentous nature in the history of Magadha, I hope you will permit me to dwell at length on this topic.

Ajātaśatru and the Lichchavis

Ajātaśatru was not on friendly terms with the Lichchavis with whom he was connected on the maternal side. He must have felt that the Lichchavis formed the greatest bar to the realisation of his ideas of an empire, and he vowed, "I will root out these Vajjians, mighty and powerful though they be; I will destroy these Vajjians; I will bring upon these Vajjians utter ruin"[2]. He was also under the impression that his foster-brother, Abhaya, who had also Lichchavi blood in him and who liked them very much might be supported by them in which case his throne might be threatened.

This is how the *Sumaṅgala-vilāsinī* speaks of the incident[3], There was a port near the Ganges extending over a *yojana*, half of which belonged to Ajātaśatru and the other half to the Lichchavis and their orders were obeyed within their respective boundaries. There was a mountain not far from it, and at the foot of the mountain, there was a mine of precious substances. Ajātaśatru was late in going there, and the avaricious

1 *The Early History of India*, p. 37. "The establishment of supremacy over Kāśi, Kośala and Videha was probably the work of his son and successor, Ajātaśatru in the first half of the fifth century". *The Cambridge History of India*, Vol, 1. 415.

2 *The Sacred Books of the East* XI. 12. Cf. also *Buddhist India*, p. 12 Also *Dialogues of the Buddha*, p. 78.

3 I am indebted to Dr. B. C. Law's learned work, *Kṣatriya Clans in Buddhist India* for this occount, as well as certain other references. *Vide* also Mr. Law's *Some Kṣatriya Tribes of Ancient India*, p. 106.

Lichchavis took away all the precious substances. When Ajātaśatru came and learnt that all the precious substances had been taken away by the Lichchavis, he grew angry aud left the place. This happened also in the succeeding year. Having sustained a heavy loss, he thought that there must be a fight between him and the Lichchavis. He realised, however, that the Lichchavis being numerically stronger, he would fail to carry out his purpose. So he conceived the design of destroying the independence of the Lichchavis by sowing among them the seeds of dissension. Formerly, the Lichchavis were not luxurious, but were very strenuous and energetic, and so Ajātaśatru could not get an opportunity of subduing them. He sent Vassakāra, one of his ministers, to the Buddha, who predicted that in future the Lichchavis would be delicate, having soft hands and feet, would use very luxurious and soft beds with soft pillows made of cotton, and would sleep till sunrise. He further declared, " By no other means will the Vajjians be overcome but by propitiating them with tributes or dissolving the subsisting union". Vassakāra returned from the Buddha and repeated his declaration to the king, Ajātaśatru. He, of course, did not like to propitiate the Vajjians with tributes, as that would diminish the number of his elephants and horses. So he decided to break their union, and Vassakāra advised him to convene a meeting of his councillors to bring up some discussions regarding the Vajjians, when in the midst of the sitting, he (Vassakāra) would quit the council after offering a remonstrance saying, "Mahārāja, what do you want with them? Let them occupy themselves with the agriculture and commercial affairs of their own (realms)." Then he said to Ajātaśatru, "Mahārāja, completely cut of all my hair, bringing charge against me for interdicting your discussion without either binding or flogging me. As I am the person by whom the ramparts and ditches of your capital were made and as I know the strong and the weak, high and low parts (of your fortifications), I will tell the Vajjians that I am able to remove any obstacle you can raise."

The Rājā acted up to the advice of his minister, Vassakāra. The Vajjians heard of the departure of Vassakāra, and some of them decided not to allow him to cross the river, while others observed : " Ve (Ajāta-śatru) has so treated him because he advocated our cause". Such being the case, they said (to the guards who went to stop him), "Fellows, let him come". Accordingly, the guards permitted him to go in.

Now Vassakāra, being questioned by the Vajjians, told them why he was so severely punished for so slight an offence, and that he was there a Judicial Prime Minister. Then the Vajjians offered him the same post which he accepted, and very soon he acquired reputation for his able administration of justice ; and the youths of the Vajji rulers went to him to have their training at his hands.

Vassakāra on a certain day, taking aside one of the Lichchavi rulers mysteriously asked him : " Do people plough a field ?" 'Yes they do ; by coupling a pair of bullocks together". On another occasion, taking another Lichchavi aside, he significantly asked : "With what curry did you eat (your rice)?" and said no more. But hearing the answer, he communicated it to another person. Then upon a subsequent occasion, taking another Lichchavi aside he asked him in a whisper, "Art thou a mere beggar ?" He enquired, "Who said so ?" and Vassakāra replied, "That Lichchavi". Again, upon another occassion, taking another aside, he enquired, "Art thou a cowherd ?", and on being asked who said so, mentioned the name of some other Lichchavi. Thus by speaking something to one person, which had not been said by another person, he succeeded in bringing about a disunion among the rulers in course of three years so completely that none of them would tread the same path together. When matters stood thus, he caused the tocsin to be sounded as usual. Some of the Lichchavi rulers disregarded the call saying, "Let the rich and the valiant assemble. We are beggars and cowherds." The Brāhmin sent a mission to the Rājā saying, "This is the proper time. Let him come quickly". The Rājā on hearing the announcement assembled his forces by beat of drum and started. The Vajjians, on receiving intimation thereof, sounded the tocsion declaring, "Let us not allow the Rājā to cross the river." On hearing this also, they refused to meet together saying, "Let the valiant rulers go". Again the tocsin was sounded and it was thus declared, "Let us defend ourselves with closed gates." No one responded to the call. Ajātaśatru entered by the wide open gates and went back, after inflicting on the people great calamities[1], Thus Magadha became master of the Lichchavis and Ajātaśatru erected a fortress on the northern bank of the Son near its confluence with the Ganges, to watch his Lichchavi opponents. Here was the beginning of the greatness of Pāṭaliputra[2].

Defeat of the Lichchavis

Greek accounts

Mahāpadma Nanda, the son of the last Saiśunāga king, Mahānandin,[3] and a Śūdra woman, established the next dynasty in or about 413 B. C.[4] Not only

1 The late Dr. Rhys Davids did not believe in this. He said, "We can only hope this ghastly story of dishonour, treachery and slaughter is a fairy tale". *The Cambridge History of India*, Vol. I. p. 185. It cannot, however, be denied that Ajātaśatru captured the stronghold of the Lichchavis.

2 See *The Early History of India*, p. 38 & f. n. I. Buddhist writers say that Udayin (who founded the Capital Pāṭaliputra) was the son and successor of Ajātaśatru. Nandi-Vardhana succeeded Udayin, according to the Purāṇas and was followed by Mahānandin.

3 *The Early History of India*, p. 41.

4 *Vide* V. A. Smith, the *Early History of India*, p. 41. where the date has been changed to 413 B. C. from 372 B. C. (third edition).

according to the *Purāṇas* but also according to two Greek accounts, he was the son of a woman of a very low status[1] who was probably one of the domestic attendants of the palace. One of the Greek accounts is by Diodorous Siculus who says: "Alexander had learned from Phegeus that beyond the Indus was a vast desert of twelve days' journey, and at the furthest borders thereof, ran the Ganges. Beyond this river dwell the Tabenians and the Gangaridae whose king's name was Chandramas, who had an army of 20,000 horse, 2,00,000 foot, 2,000 chariots, and 4,000 elephants. The king could not believe this to be true and sent for Poros and enquired of him whether it was so or not. He told him all was certainly true, but that the present king of the Gangaridae was but of mean and obscure extraction, accounted to be a barber's son; for his father being a very handsome man, the queen fell in love with him and murdered her husband and so the kingdom devolved upon the present king"[2].

The other accounts given by Quintus Curtius who notes: "Poros added, however, that the king was not only of low, but of extremely base origin, for his father was a barber whose personal merits recommended him to the queen. Being introduced by her to the king then reigning, he contrived to bring about his death, and under pretence of acting as guardian to his sons got them into his power and put them to death. After their extermination, he begot the son who was now king, and who, more worthy of his father's condition than his own, was odious and contemptible to his subjects".

Dr. Keith considered 372 B. C. as being put too high, "if he is to be taken as alive at the time of Alexander."

1 *J. B. & O. R. S.*, I. 88 & IV. 91.

2 Diodorus, XVII. Chap. 93 : Curtius, IX. Chap. 2.

Being a son of the king, Mahāpadma must have had, in accordance with the usual custom of Hindu royalty, access to the royal household and was naturally entrusted with the guardianship of the princes. During the regency of Mahāpadma, which lasted for eight years, the princes died, whereupon he ascended the throne[1].

Nava-Nandas

The Nava-Nandas or the Neo-Nandas[2] were followed by the Mauryas—Chandragupta, the founder, the Sandracottos of the Greek writers[3], who was placed on the throne by Chāṇakya Viṣṇugupta. Bindusāra or Amrita-Khāda[4] and Asoka, the *Rāja Chakravarti*, of whose Edicts we will speak in our third and fourth lectures, followed[5]. Then a few others came, under whom Magadha not only ceased to be the premier state of India, but the tables were turned; for Kaliṅga which had acknowledged the suzerainty of Asoka, became prominent under Khāravela, the aggressive Jain king[6], who in the twelfth year of his

1 *J. B.* & *O. R. S.* I. 88.

2 Cf. *Ibid*, p. 87. Mr. Jayaswal would call them Neo Nandas. *J. B. & O. R. S.*, IV. 91. "The Neo-Nanda theory of Mr. Jayaswal", Dr. Keith observes, "is a most unplausible guess." See also *The Early History of India*, p. 44 f. n. According to the Purāṇas, the Nandas represent no new family; they are the direct descendants of the Śisunāgas, the last and the last but one of whom, Mahānandin the Nandivardhana bear names which indicate their connection." *The Cambridge History of India*, Vol. I, 313.

3 This identification first established the "sheet anchor" of ancient Indian chronology. "The identity, recognised by William Jones, of the Indian Chandragupta and the Sandracottos of the historians of Alexander, remains the cornerstone of all Indian chronology. During a period of a thousand years, the history of India is to a great extent the history of the knowledge possessed by the Greeks concerning India" Levi in *Ancient India*. According to H. R. Dev, *J. B. & O. R. S.*, IV. 91, Chandragupta Maurya was a kinsman of the respectable early Nandas and not a Sudra or lowcasteman, like the later Nandas of ill-repute.

4 Bindusāra seems to have made his authority felt in the Deccan perhaps as far south as the latitude of Madras.

5 *See J. R. A. S.*, 1911, 943 ff.

6 *J. B. & O. R. S.*, Vol. I., 166 ff., V. H. Jackson, on *Two new inscriptions from the Barabar Hills, and an identification of*

Gorathagiri Inscription.
(Figure No. 1)

The Same (Figure No. 2)

To face p. 25.

A Sunga Inscription.
(Ayodhya—Ranupali Inscription)

To face p. 25.

reign caused "consternation amongst the people of Magadha" and made the king render him homage. The Suṅgas commencing with Puṣyamitra[1], revived the *Aśvamedha*. The Kaṇvas[2] who codified the *Manu Saṁhitā*, caused the *Bhāṣyas* to be written on the philosophical *Sūtras*, recast the *Mahābhārata*, and the *Rāmāyaṇa* to their present shape, compiled the *Nātyaśāstras* from the previous literature on the subject and even

---

Gorathagiri Vol. III. p. 432. *J. R. A. S.*, 1913, p. 543, V. A. Smith's *New Light on Ancient India*. Rai Bahadur R. Chanda, *Date of Khāravela* in *I. A.*, 1919, p. 214. Also *Ibid*, *Second note on the Hāthigumphā Inscription of Khāravela*, p. 187 by Dr. R. C. Majumdar. See also V. H. Jackson in *J. B. & O. R. S.*, XII. The date of the first invasion of Khāravela was c. 165 B. C. The second which was more successful can be dated at 161 B. C. According to Barnett, *Antiquities of India*, 41, "Khāravila, son of Vṛiddha-rāja and grandson of Kṣhema-rājā succeeded to the throne of Kaliṅga about 155. Sometime afterwards he, with the aid of Yajna-sena Sātakarṇi, penetrated into Magadha, and apparently forced Pushyamitra to seek peace."

1 The drama, *Mālavikāgnimitra* by Kālidāsa gives a good idea of some of the events of this reign. According to Mahāmahopadhyāya H. P. Sastri, *J. A. S. B.*, VI, 260, "Puṣya Mitra belonged perhaps to these turbulent military spirits who had been driven away from Persia by the Greek conquest of that country, for the second half of his name, Mitra, and that of all the members of his family show his Persian origin. He was a Brāhminist to the core and hated the Buddhists". According to Bühler. *I. A.*, II. 262, both Puṣpamitra and Puṣyamitra are correct. For *Some observations on Puṣyamitra and his Empire* by Dr. R. C. Majumdar, see the *Journal of Indian History*. I. *Vide*, also *J. B. & O. R. S., X. Puṣyamitra, who is he*, see *Third Oriental Conference, Madras, 1924.*

The Brāhmin dynasty which uprooted the Buddhist Mauryas and succeeded to the imperial throne of India about 188 B.C. brought an orthodox revolution in literature and Hindu society. The dynasty adopted the *Gotra* name Suṅga as its title. Kālidāsa mentions the *Aśvamedha* of Puṣyamitra and makes his daughter-in-law refer to him as *Senāpati*, a fact mentioned by the Purāṇas, according to which he was the chief of the military department of the Mauryas. Two *Aśvamedhas* are referred to and Mr. Jayaswal thinks that as he was defeated by Khāravela, evidently after his first sacrifice, he re-established his imperial position a second time. *J. B. & O. R. S., X* 205. The two *Aśvamedhas* may be a challenge, as it were, to the *Ahiṁsā* doctrine of Aśoka, who had prohibited *Samāja* in his edicts. *Vide* Lectures III & IV.

2 *J. A. S. B.*, May, 1910. The Kāṇva dynasty was founded about 72 B. C. (according to Dr. Barnett) when Deva-bhumi, the last Suṅga-king, perished through a plot instigated by the Brāhman minister Vasu-Deva who became the founder.

brought about the codification of the *Kāmaśāstra* from the pre-existing material, then came in. The Andhras[1] followed, but so far as rank and fame were concerned, Magadha practically ceased to enjoy any.[2]

Not only that. During the Kuṣān dynasty the very centre of Magadha, Pāṭaliputra, was attacked, and it may be that during the time of Huviṣka and Vāsudeva, Magadha was part and parcel of the Kuṣān empire.[3] After the Kuṣāns, we have nothing on record

1 According to *The Cambridge History of India*, Vol I. 317, "The Suṅgas, Kaṇvas and Andhras were contemporary, although no doubt they claimed the suzerainty of N. India successively. That the first two of these were ruling at the same time may be inferred from the incidental statement that the first Andhra king destroyed the last of the Kaṇvas and "what was left of the Suṅgas' power." (*Kali Age*, pp. 38, 71)......"Both powers, Suṅga and Andhra alike, arose on the ruins of the Maurya empire—the former in the Midland Country and the latter in Southern India." "It was probably not until the reign of the third Andhra king, Sātakarṇi, that they came into collision; and then their political association appears to have been transient." *Ibid*, p. 318. The Purāṇas, however, have a different story.

2 It is a debatable point whether the Andhras had really any connexion with Magadha. "Their only possible claim to a place in its records must have been founded on a conquest which transferred to them the suzerainty previously held by Magadha." *The Cambridge History of India*, Vol. I, p. 318 "The Āndhra dynasty was founded about 220 B. C. by Simuka. Its seat was the Telegu country, in the deltas of the Godāveri and Kistna, of which the capital was Sri-Kākulam." *Antiquities of India*, 40.

3 This view of Mr. R. D. Banerjee is, however, open to doubt. The evidence he has put forward in his Bengalee *History of Bengal*, Vol. I, p. 36, is (1) that a cast of a coin of Huviṣka was discovered at the foot of the Bodhi tree when the temple was being repaired (Cunningham, *Mahābodhi*, p. 20, plate VII). The finding of a mere cast is hardly evidence enough to come to a definite conclusion like the above: and (2) that Mr. J. D. Beglar, while engaged in the reconstruction of the Mahābodhi, discovered a Bodhisatva figure of the Mathurā red-stone. (Cunningham, *Mahābodhi*, pp. (17—21, plate XXV). Mr. Banerjee *surmises* that the piece of sculpture was made at Mathurā and then brought to Buddha Gaya for installation. It seems hardly probable, however, that the decadent Kuṣān power, after the death of Kaniṣka, could have advanced so far. Doubts are expressed of Kaniṣka's attacking the Magadhan king at Pāṭaliputra, and it can hardly be accepted as true that his successors, who were certainly less powerful, could have ventured to come so far, though Mr. V. A. Smith was of opinion that "there are grounds for the belief that from the time of Kaniṣka to the reign of Vāsudeva, Kuṣān rule extended over Bihar." See also *J. B. & O. R. S.*, VI, 22. For the date of Kaniṣka, see, *Indian Historical Quarterly*, Vol. I., 415 ff.

Coin representing the marriage of Chandra Gupta with Kumara Devi.

To face p. 27.

to be able to say who ruled over Magadha,—there was indeed a blank till the Imperial Guptas came.

The Guptas

The marriage of Chandra Gupta I with Kumāra Devī was a momentous event, a fact so often and so clearly mentioned in the Gupta Inscriptions. It was evidently in consequence of this marriage of the Mahādevi with the local Gupta king that Magadha again rose in splendour and re-established its lost power. So far as the conquests of Samudra Gupta are concerned, we are now familiar with practically every detail. Volume III of Fleet's important and interesting work gives us many details of the Gupta Emperors, while the valuable Introduction to Mr. John Allan's *Catalogue of the Coins of the Gupta Dynasties* gives us a good account of the same dynasty. Mr. Vincent A. Smith's well-merited labours to elucidate this period have also to be mentioned. Nor can we forget our debt of gratitude to Dr. S. K. Aiyangar for his successful attempts and for his systematic study of the Gupta period. Dr. R. Shāmaśástri who has already done us so great a service by his discovery and translation of Chāṇakya's *Artha-śāstrā* has further rendered us help by his exhaustive and learned discourse on the age of the early Guptas[1].

Samudra Gupta

It is not possible to go into detail, but I am sure you will permit me to refer to the conquest in the extreme south by Samudra Gupta the earliest invasion of which any historical record is available, if we leave out of account the more or less mythological expedition to the *Dākṣinātya*[2] by the epic hero, Rāma Chandra, thus showing the way, a thousand years afterwards for the Muhammadan King, Alauddin, and his still more

1 *Annual Report of the Mysore Archaeological Department, 1923.*

2 *Vide the Indian Historical Quarterly*, I. 2, *Identification of the Princes and Territories mentioned in the Allahabad Pillar Inscription* by D. R. Bhandarkar and I. 4, *Kingdoms of the Deccan*, by G. Ramdas.

successful captain, Malik Kafur. I shall also refer to the very curious piece of sculpture—an inscribed stone-horse of this great hero, "who by his sharp and polished intellect and choral skill and musical accomplishments established his title of "King of poets", by various poetical compositions that were fit to be the means of subsistence of learned people," now adorning the Lucknow Museum[1], representing the *Aśvamedha* sacrifice of the "Indian Napoleon", though this title is rather improperly given, for he had certainly a nobler aim than being merely a "Napoleon who regarded kingdom-taking as the duty of kings."[2] The fact that Samudra Gupta actually performed this solemn rite—it is interesting to note from the Inscription of Chandra Gupta II that Samudra Gupta *restored* this sacrifice—is vouched for by his inscription as well as by the *Aśvamedha* coins, or rather medals, which are very rare, and of which only three specimens have been discovered in Magadha up to the present time. This sculpture is the life-size figure in stone of a horse which was discovered some years ago near the ancient fort of Khairigarh in the Kheri district between the boundaries of Oudh and Nepal. In his old age, Samudra Gupta had the story of the conquest written by his court poet, Harisena, and had it engraved on the Aśoka pillar at Allahabad, thus enabling the historian to define the boundaries of the great king's dominions with sufficient accuracy and to realize the nature of the political divisions of India in the fourth century.[3]

---

1 Allahabad Inscription. Cf. also Mathurā Inscription cf Chandra Gupta II. For the Gupta pillar at Bihar, see *J. B. & O. R. S.*, V. 64.

2 *The Early History of India*, p. 306.

3 For *Indian Administration in the age of the Guptas* (300-700 A.D.), see Radha Kumud Mookerjee, *Journal of Indian History*, Sept., 1925.

Then followed the later Gupta dynasty,[1] the kings of which appear to have been for the most part merely local rulers of Magadha though the most notable of them, Ādityasena, presumed to celebrate the horse-sacrifice in token of his claim to supreme rank. The last known king of the dynasty was Jīvita Gupta II who reigned early in the eighth century. Along with the Later Guptas, the Maukhari dynasty[2] whose existence near or at Buddha Gaya can be traced back to the 3rd or the 2nd century B. C., and whose rule over the country around Buddha Gaya during the sixth and seventh centuries is well known to us from inscriptions and literary works, very likely shared Magadha with the Later Guptas. It is also interesting to note that, although during this period, Magadha had ceased to be the head-quarters of any Imperial power and had sunk into insignificance, its reputation as the centre and head-quarters of Buddhistic learning did not cease, and it even then attracted scholars. In 527, Wu-ti or Hsiao Yen, the first Liang emperor of China and an ardent Buddhist, sent a mission to Magadha for the purpose of collecting original *Mahāyānist* texts and obtaining the services of a scholar competent to translate them. Indeed, the Gupta period consisting of more than three centuries and a half was a time of exceptional intellectual activity in many fields—a time, as Mr. V. A. Smith has rightly observed, "not unworthy of comparison with the Elizabethan and Stuart periods in England"[3]. In

Later Guptas

1 For *Later Gupta History and Chronology*, see the *Journal of Indian History*, IV. 2. Also *I. A.*, 1918, p. 161, *The Revised Chronology of the Last Gupta Emperors* by Dr. R. C. Majumdar.

2 *Indian Antiquary*, IX. 178 : Also, *J. R. A. S.*, New Series VI., 141. Mr. N. G. Majumdar is responsible for the conclusion that from the Harāhā Inscription it is clear that the extensive conquests of Isanavarman were achieved during the reign of his father Iśvaravarman who, accordingly, must be regarded as the first Maukhari to have attained an imperial status.

3 *The Early History of India*, p. 322. Dr. Barnett said, "The

Literature, Science, Architecture, Sculpture, Painting and Die-cutting everything was perfect, due not only to the personal patronage of the kings but to contact with foreign civilisation, both in the east and in the west.

The Pālas

Early in the eighth century a chieftain named Gopāla was *elected* king of Bengal. The state of the country since 730 was a deplorable one. The king of Assam had conquered the greater part of eastern India and Gauḍ is mentioned by name as one of the countries held by the king in subjection[1]. Vatsarāja, the Gurjara king, acquired the sovereignity of another portion, sometime about 760 A. D[2]. It was at this juncture that Gopāla "the son of Vapyata, crest-jewel of the heads of kings, the glorious one, whom the people made take the hand of fortune, to put an end to the practice of fishes[3], whose everlasting great fame the glorious mass of moonlight on a full-moon night seeks to rival by its witness in the sky", became the king of Bengal[4]. Thus was established the Pāla dynasty[5] which conquered Magadha. Gopāla's

---

Gupta period is in the annals of classical India almost what the Periclean age is in the history of Greece." *J. R. A. S.*, 1917, p. 417.

1 *Indian Antiquary*, IX, p. 78.

2 *Rāmacharita*, p. 3.

3 *Mātsya Nyāya.* Chāṇakya has clearly explained this term, in his *Arthaśāstra.* It also occurs in the *Mahābhārata*, Sānti Parvan. For the chronology of the Pāla Kings, see *J. A. S. B.*, New Series, Vol. XVII, 1921, p. I ff, the article by Dr. R. C. Majumdar. Cf. also *I. A.*, 1920, p. 189, *A Chronology of the Pāla Dynasty of Bengal*, by D. C. Bhattacharya. For inscriptions relating to the Pāla period, see Nilmani Chakravarti, *Pāla Inscriptions in the Indian Museum*, *J. A. S. B.*, IV (1908, pp. 101 ff).

4 Tāranāth says that Gopāla began to rule in Bengal and afterwards reduced Magadha.

5 Khālimpur Plate, *Epigraphia Indica*, IV. 251, Tāranāth, the Tibetan historian also refers to this *election* of Gopāla, by the people. He tells us how the wife of one of the kings by night assassinated every one of those who had been chosen to be kings, but after a certain number of years, the king delivered himself from her and was made king for life. Tāranāth, p. 216 says, "After him, Dharmapāla was *chosen* as ruler. He reigned for 64 years and as he had also brought Kāmarupa, Tirhut and Gauḍ under his subjection, his dominion was very large." For an *Account of the Successive Events in the Reign of Dharmapāladeva, see J. B. & O. R. S.*, XII, 361 ff.

son was Dharmapāla, the *Parama-saugata Parameśvara Paramabhaṭṭāraka Mahārājādhirāja*[1] "whose achievements are praised by the good, a master of kings who alone is the sole ruler of the entire earth ; whose progress, when he is about to conquer the quarters all round, the four oceans, marked by the footprints of the array of his elephants that bathe on their shores, patiently permit being no longer fosses on the earth", who installed the illustrious king of Kānyakubja, who readily was accepted by the Bhoja, Matsya, Madra, Kuru, Yadu, Yavana, Avanti, Gandharva and Kirāt kings bowing down respectfully with their diadems trembling and for whom his own golden coronation jar was lifted up by the delighted elders of Pañchāla." All these we learn from the Khālimpur grant[2] attested to by the Bhagalpur plate[3]. King Dharmapāla was a man of exceptional capacity and a devout Buddhist, bestowing liberal patronage on learned teachers and numerous monastic communities, and was the founder of the famous Vikramaśilā University, of which we shall speak in our sixth lecture. The popularity of this Prince who issued his grant from Pāṭaliputra "where the manifold fleets of boats proceeding on the path of the Bhāgīrathī made it seem as if a series of mountain tops had been sunk to build another causeway," can be estimated when we read that his praises were sung by cowherds on the borders, by foresters in the forests, by villagers on the outskirts of villages, by groups of playing children in every courtyard, in every market, by the guardians of the weights and in pleasure-houses,

Dharmapāla

1 Cf. also *Indian Antiquary*, Vol. XXI; also *Gauḍa Lekhamālā* 11 ff. Cf. also, *Indian Antiquary*, XV. 304 and XX. 308; *Epigraphia Indica*, IV. Also Tod, *Rajasthan*, edited by G. H. Ojha, p. 533.

2 *Epigraphia Indica*, IV. 252. According to Tāranāth p. 216, Dharmapāla was also *chosen* as a ruler. He reigned, as the Tibetan historian observes, for 64 years, and brought Gauḍ under his subjection.

3 *I. A.*, XV, 304 & XX, 304.

by the parrots in the cages[1]. Dharamapāla restored Buddhism, but he was tolerant of Hinduism[2]. His Mahāsammata established a big *Viṣṇumandir* at a place called Subbasthalī, and in the twenty-sixth year of his reign, on the fifth day of the dark fortnight of the month of *Bhādra*, on a Saturday, a *liṅgam* with four faces was set up in the pleasant abode of the Lord of Dharma by Keśava, the stone-cutter, for the descendants of Snātakas who lived at Mahābodhi[3]. The Khālimpur grant is also a proof of his toleration.

Another king of the same dynasty with whom Magadha was intimately connected was Devapāla[4] the worthy son of Dharmapāla. I say, intimately, for an inscription of Devapāla, as it is on record, was issued from Monghyr[5], while his Nālandā copper-plate is also important.[6]

We have already spoken of Dharmapāla, the greatest king of the Pāla dynasty, and of his toleration, and similar proofs of toleration of other kings of this line are not wanting. The copper plate of Madanapāla also testifies to the above. This grant to a Brāhmaṇa by this Buddhist king was made as a *dakṣiṇā* or honorarium for having read the *Mahābhārata* to his queens. This is one more fact showing the toleration of the Buddhist kings of the Pāla dynasty and the intimate connection

1 *Epi. Ind.*, IV. 252.

2 Cf. Devapāla's Inscription, *Indian Antiquary*, Vol. XXX.

3 See *Mahābodhi*, pl. XXVIII, 3: Also Proceedings of *A. S. B.*, 1880 and Journal and Proceedings of *A. S. B.*, Vol. IV (New Series), pp. 101-102. Also *A. S. R.*, 1908, article by Dr. Bloch.

4 Cf. *J. A. S. B.*, LXIII (1894), p. 41. According to some, Devapāladeva was the mightiest member of the Pāla dynasty: *J. B. & O. R. S.*, XII, 361.

5 *Asiatic Researches*, Vol. 1; *Indian Antiquary*, XXI. Prof. S. N. Majumdar Sāstri has brought to light a new inscription of Devapāla which we shall refer to in our fifth Lecture. *J. B.* & *O. R. S.*, X. 37.

6 *Vide Epigraphia Indica*, XVII, *The Nālandā Copperplate of Devapāladeva* by H. Sastri.

that existed at the time between Buddhism and Hinduism—one of the reasons which led to the easy downfall of the former, when Magadha was invaded by the Muhammadans. The decay and destruction of Buddhism will be discussed in a subsequent lecture.

Their Capital

Where was, however, the capital of the Pāla kings? Mahāmahopādhyāya Haraprasād Sāstri is of opinion that they had no capitals[1], that they lived in camps only, and wandered about from one place to another. The Khālimpur Inscription[2] was issued from Pāṭaliputra, mentioned in the *Praśasti* as a "Victorious Camp", and Devapāla issued his grant from Monghyr[3] but in none is mentioned the capital of these kings who were so very powerful. Can this be possible? Mr. Akṣaya Kumar Maitreya, C. I. E., the well-known scholar and Director of the *Vārendra Research Society*, took great offence at the above suggestion of the learned Sāstri and questioned whether it was possible for such powerful kings to have had no capital, no fixed place of habitation and to have been like wandering gipsies. But Mr. Maitreya has not himself suggested the name of any place and has contented himself only by mentioning that proofs of the Pāla kings having had their capital will be given in a subsequent volume of the publications of the *Vārendra Research Society*. Up to this time inscriptions of the second, third, fifth, ninth, eleventh and seventeenth kings of the dynasty have been discovered, and it is indeed curious[4] that in none of these there has been any mention

1 *Rāmacharita*, p. 6.

2 *J. A. S. B.*, LX III, part I, p. 39 and *E. I.*, IV. 243.

3 See *I. A.*, XXI, 254-257, *Mungir Copper plate Grant* of Devapāla by Prof. E. Keilhorn. The Professor observed it as the first Sanskrit inscription that was ever brought to the notice of Sanskrit scholars.

4 Mr. E. H. Walsh in his Foreword to *Rambles in Bihar* says, "The town of Bihar was the capital of the Pāla dynasty which ruled

of their capital. Strange indeed! In the absence of any other proof it would be unjustifiable to hazard any definite conclusion; but considering that the Khālimpur *Praśasti* refers to Pāṭaliputra as the Victory Camp and that both the Devapāla inscriptions, one discovered at Monghyr and the other at Nālandā refer to Śrīnagar[1] which has been identified with Pāṭaliputra, can it be that the "Victory Camp" at Pāṭaliputra of Dharmapāla was made the capital by his successor Devapāla? This seems to me, until the discovery of some proof to the contrary, a not-altogether unacceptable conclusion.

Two other Pāla kings also deserve more than a passing notice. Mahīpāla[2] the ninth sovereign whose dates can be assigned to a period between 978-1030, is very well known, and who may be assumed to have won back his ancestral throne and with whose name are associated the Mahīpāla songs. It was in his time that Paṇḍita Dharmapāla and other holy men from Magadha accepted the invitation from Tibet to restore Buddhism. This was followed by the mission of Atiśa, of whom we shall speak later on. The other king was Rāmapāla whose history has been given in the *Rāmacharita* discovered by M. M. Haraprasād Sāstri[3]. The importance of this history of Bengal in the second half of the eleventh and the first half of the twelfth centuries cannot be exaggerated. As the learned Mahāmahopādhyāya observes: "It is a contemporary record though obscured by double

Rāma-charita

Magadha and Bengal for over two hundred years from the ninth to the twelfth centuries."

1 Could, however, Śrīnagar mean, Chief Town, whatever that chief town may be? V. A. Smith says, Dharmapāla, the most powerful of the Pāla kings of Bengal and Bihar, evidently took some steps to renew the glory of Pāṭaliputra, because we know that in the thirty-second year of his reign (about A.D. 811) he had his court there. *E.H.I.*, 311.

2 Portions of Magadha, if not the whole of it, was in the occupation of the Pratihāras, till Mahīpāla I annexed Magadha to his territories. *The Pālas of Bengal*, p. 59; also *I. A.*, 1908, p. 109.

3 Published by the Asiatic Society of Bengal as one of its Memoirs, Vol. III, No. 1.

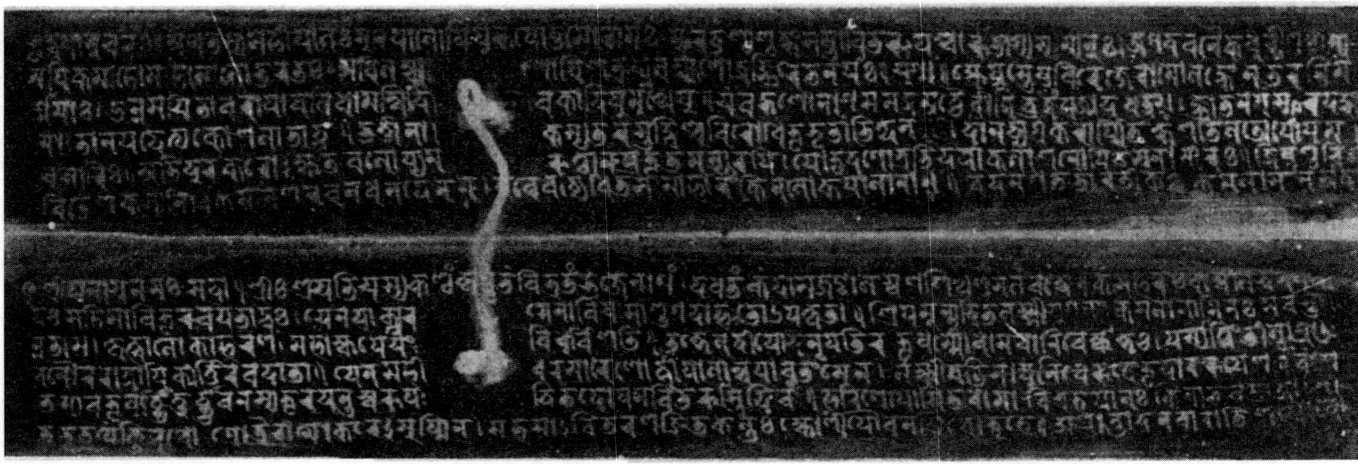

Pages from Ramacharita.

To face p. 34.

en tendre, and as such records are so rare for India, and specially for the eastern portion of it, that it may be pronounced as unique"[1]. Though the inscriptions bring before us five more kings of their time, Rāmapāla may be considered as the last who exercised considerable power.[2]

Very likely in 1160 had been reigning in Magadha one Govindapāla Deva, in the fourth year of whose reign was copied an *Aṣṭasāhasrikā Prajñāpāramitā*[3]. Who this Govindapāla was and to which Pāla dynasty he belonged, it is difficult to ascertain. He had as his title, *Parameśvara Paramabhaṭṭāraka Māhārāj adhirāja Paramasaugata*, the last whereof indicates that he was also a Buddhist. His reign is mentioned in the Inscription in the temple of *Gadādhara*[4] at Gayā. There are references to his reign in old manuscripts as well, *e.g.*, in the copy of the *Prajñāpāramitā*[5], in the library of the Asiatic Society of Bengal, as well as in a copy of *Guhyāvalī Vivṛti* in Cambridge University[6]. In the thirty-eighth year of his reign there is a reference to his having lost his kingdom[7]. This was the year when Magadha was invaded by the Muhammadans. Govindapāla was weak. With the aid of the monks[8] he tried to defend the fort on the hill where was situated the Vihār of Odandapura. Govindapāla was defeated and killed. From that time the existence of Magadha as a separate

Muslim Invasion

1 Introduction to *Rāmacharita*, p. 2.

2 The chief authority for the Pāla period is Mr. R. D. Banerjee's, *The Pālas of Bengal*, but his views have to be accepted cautiously.

3 *J. R. A. S.*, Vol. III (1876), p. 3.

4 *A. S. R.*, Vol. III, 125.

5 *J. A. S. B.*, 1893, p. 1.

6 *Catalogue of Buddhist Sanskrit Manuscripts*, Cambridge.

7 R. D. Banerjee, *The Pālas of Bengal*. The authority of the Pālas had been already shaken by the Kāmboja usurpation in the latter part of the tenth century and again by the Kaivarta rising in the eleventh century. V. A. Smith, *The Early History of India*, 41.

8 This is based on Tāranāth.

kingdom ceased practically[1]. Along with Magadha, Bengal also shared her fall. The Sena dynasty founded by Sāmanta Sena was swept away by the torrent of Muhammadan invasion at the end of the twelfth century. Not long after the easy conquest of Bihar, Muhammad, the son of Bakhtiyar, invaded Bengal, of which Nudiah was then the capital with Rājā Lakṣmana Sena as its King. Muhammad appeared suddenly and the Rājā who was at his dinner fled barefooted by the rear of the palace[2].

As has been established now, the early Muslim invasions were mere incursions. The Jānibighā inscription[4] shows that the rule of the Sena kings continued in some parts of Magadha after the first Muhammadan invasion. This stone inscription, which is now in the Patna Museum, is of very great importance in the history of the Sena epoch. It is dated in the era of Lakṣmana Sena[5], the year being 83, *i. e.* the third year, 1202, after the Muhammadan expedition. This inscription now proves beyond doubt that though a portion of Bihar was conquered, the neighbouring district of Gayā remained under a scion of the Sena family in the time of Muhammad Ibn Bakhtiyar[5].

1 For the fall of the Pālas, see *J. A. S. B.*, 1911, p. 615. "The Pālas seem to have held Magadha or South Bihar and Munghir in North Bihar, almost throughout the end, with little interruption, but during the last century of this rule they lost nearly the whole of Bengal to the Senas." *The Early Histovy of India*, p. 147. See also *J. B. & O. R. S.*, Vol. V., part II, 295-297.

2 See Tabakāt-i-Nāsri, Ravetri's edition, p 552. For the chronology of the Sena Kings, see *J. A. S. B.*, New Series, XVII, 1921, article by Dr. R. C. Majumdar, pp. 7 ff. See also V. A. Smith, *The Early History of India*, pp. 431 ff.

3 *J. B. & O. R. S.*, Vol. IV. I may be pardoned for claiming some credit in having secured it for the Patna Museum.

4 During the reign of Lakṣmana Sena, the western part of Magadha seems to have passed into the hands of the Gāhaḍavāla kings of Kanauj. *The Pālas of Bengal*, p. 107.

5 *J. B. & O. R. S.*, Vol. IV, 266. See also *The Indian Antiquary* XL VIII, p. 43 (article by N. G. Majumdar).

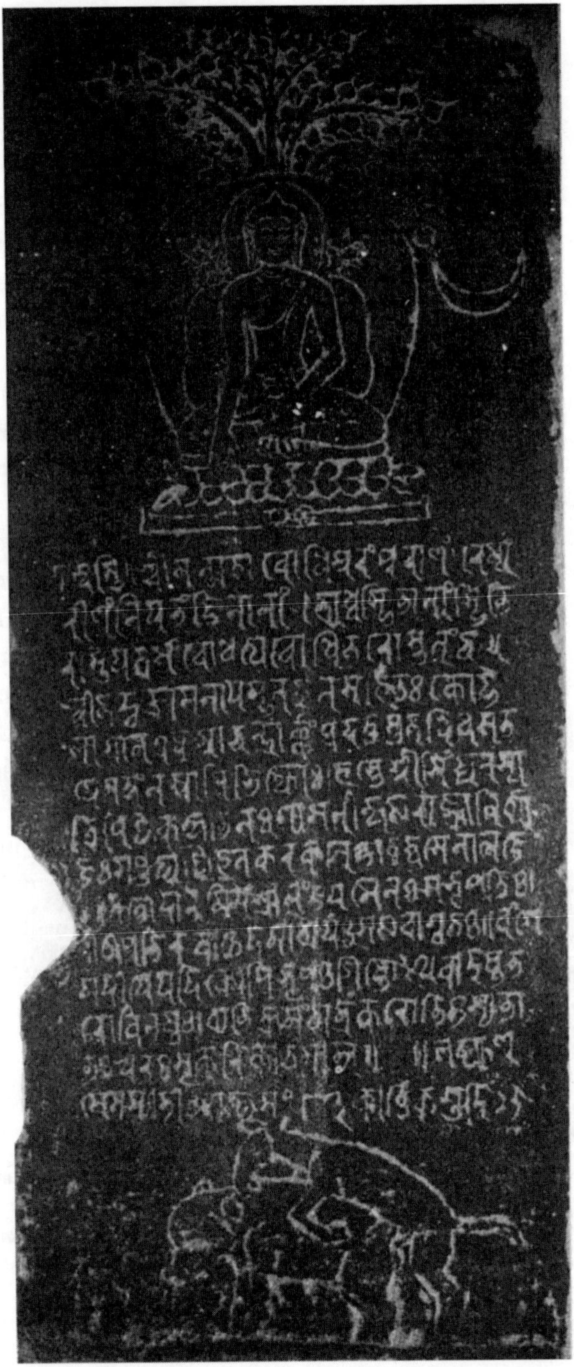

This fact, along with that of Rājā Indradyumna[1] ruling over some parts of Magadha would go to prove that the attack of Muhammad Bakhtyiar Khilji was of the nature of an inroad. It may, also, be mentioned that the Senas continued to exist as a local dynasty in eastern Bengal, subordinate to the Muhammadans for four generations after the capture of Nudiah[2]. But so far as Buddhism was concerned, it received its death-blow[3]. Its vitality was sapped. This we propose to discuss in one of our subsequent lectures.[4]

1 *J. B. & O. R. S.*, Vol. V., p. 295.

2 *The Early History of India*, p. 422 f. n.

3 See *J. A. S. B.*, LXIV., part I., 1895, pq 55-68.

4 Lecture VI.

LECTURE II

The Capitals of Magadha

I have already observed in my first lecture that Magadha had two capitals, first Girivraja, latterly known as Rājagṛha, and then Pāṭaliputra. I shall, in this lecture, attempt to throw some light on these two ancient cities, the stone walls of the former being very old "stone-buildings in India," the latter being very aptly called by Mahāmahopādhyāya Haraprasād Sāstri an "eternal city"[1]. Before, however, I do so, perhaps you will allow me to make a digression and refer to the question whether Vaiśālī was also once the capital of Magadha.

The claims of Vaisāli to be the Capital of Magadha

This suggestion has been fairly longstanding. More than two decades ago, Dr. Rhys Davids, the great scholar whose loss we all must always deplore, spoke of "Śiśunāga's transferring the capital to Vaiśālī"[2]. Mr. Vincent Smith, to whom all Indians are so much indebted for his labours in unearthing the glories of ancient India, observes, that "the high importance attached by the founder of the Gupta era in A. D. 320 to his alliance with the Lichchavi princess suggests that, during the third century Pāṭaliputra may have been held by the Non-Aryan Lichchavis of Vaiśālī[3]. He again refers to it elsewhere[4] when he says, "It seems probable that at the time of this fateful union (*i. e.*, the marriage of Chandra Gupta with Kumāra Devī) the Lichchavis were masters of the ancient imperial city". Turnour, also in his edition of *Mahāvaṁśa* observes, "It appears that for sometime, at least,

1 *J. B. & O. R. S.*, Vol. V.

2 *Buddhist India*, p. 37.

3 *The Early History of India*, p. 296.

4 *Ibid*, p. 295.

if not during the period of Kālāśoka's reign the capital continued to be at Vaiśālī"[1]. Let us discuss this.

The Tibetan *Dulva* gives us the following story about the marriage. "Sakala, a minister of king Virudhaka of Videha, had been obliged to flee from his country on account of the jealousy of the other ministers of the king. So he went to Vaiśalī together with his two sons, Gopāla and Simha. Sakala soon became a prominent citizen in Vaiśalī ; and, after a while, he was elected Nāyaka. His two sons married at Vaiśalī, and Simha had a daughter whom they called Vāsavi. It was foretold that she would bear a son who would take his father's life, place the crown on his own head, and seize the sovereignty for himself. Simha's wife bore him, moreover, another daughter whom they called Upavāsavi, and the soothsayers declared that she would bear a son endowed with excellent qualities. Gopāla was fierce and of great strength. So he ravaged the parks of the Lichchavis. To restrain him, the popular assembly gave him and his brother a park. When Sakala died, the people appointed Simha, his son, Nāyaka. Gopāla feeling slighted at this, departed from Vaiśalī and took up his residence at Rājagṛha in Magadha, where he became the first minister of Bimbisāra. A little later on, king Bimbisāra married Vāsabi, Gopāla's niece, and as she was of a family from Videha, she became known as Vaidehi. After a while she bore a son, who, on account of the prediction made to his father, received the name of Ajātaśatru or the enemy not yet born"[2].

Referring to this matrimonial alliance, Professor Bhandarkar of the Calcutta University, in his learned *Carmichael Lectures*[3], came to the conclusion that this was "a result of the peace concluded after the war

---

1 XXIX.

2 *Vide* Mr. B. C. Law's *Kṣatriya Clans in Buddhist India.* Also Rockhill's *Life of Buddha*, pp. 63—64.

3 1918, p. 74.

between Bimbisāra and the Lichchavis". And he further says that, "Bimbisāra thus appears to have seized Magadha after expelling the Vajjis beyond the Ganges". Dr. Bhandarkar cites, as his evidence, a passage from the *Suttanipāta*[1].

A verse occurs in the *Pārāyana*, a poem now included in the *Suttanipāta*, which referring to a time when the Buddha was alive, calls Vaiśālī a Magadha city. The great Pāli Scholar, Dr. Fausball, translated the passage referred to by Dr. Rhys Davids and Dr. Bhandarkar as follows: "And to Pāva, the city of wealth; to Vaiśālī, the city of Magadha". Dr. Bhandarkar observes: "If Vaiśālī was then the capital of the Magadha kingdom, it is quite possible that it was at the expense of the Vajjis that Bimbisāra secured territory for himself"[2].

This, as has been very well observed, "is too frail a reed on which to hang the whole theory"[3].

The only thing in support of the theory is that Vaiśālī, and, indeed, the whole Vajjian confederacy at the time when the *Mahāparinibbāna Suttanta* was put together in its present shape, was independent of Magadha, up to the Nirvāṇa of the Buddha.. "If, therefore, the reading in our text of the *Pārāyana* be correct, the expression "Magadha City" must be taken in the sense of "now a Magadha City" and as alluding to the conquest of Vaiśālī"[4] by Ajātaśatru. There might have been a war between Bimbiśāra and the Lichchavis, but it has no direct bearing on the question. Further, the commentator *Atthakathākara* interpreted the passage in the *Suttanipāta* in a way from which *Māgadha puram*

1 *Carmichael Lectures*, 1918.

2 *Ibid*, p. 73.

3 *Kṣatriya Clans in Buddhist India*, p. 127.

4 *The Cambridge History of India*, Vol. I, p. 188. Dr. Keith's reference to this is as follows: "Even if Vaiśālī was called in the *Pārayāna* a Magadhan city, it does not seem that this means that it was the capital of Magadha, but merely that it was in Magadhan territory."

evidently means the city of Magadha, *i. e.*, Rājagṛha and not Vaiśālī[1].

I shall now place before you the history of the first capital of the land we live in, *viz.*, Girivraja or Rājagṛha.

The history of Rājagṛha

According to Hardy, it was so called because not only it was founded by a king but every house in it resembled the palace *i. e.*, royal residence. It was named also Kusāgārapura or "the royal city of best grass"[2], which possesses very old[3] structural monuments of India, which can be assigned with some definiteness, to the historical period. "The beginnings of the older city are quite lost in the impenetrable mists of the earliest antiquity, but as the 'modern city' outside its gates dates from at least the sixth century B. C., it seems safe to assign the rude but massive masonry of the inner one to a period which can hardly be later than the eighth century B. C., and may be incalculably older"[4]. Girivraja was the name in the

---

1 For an account of the excavations at Basārh, see *A. S. R.*, 1903-4, where the question regarding ancient Vaiśāli and its modern sites have been also cursorily discussed. But as Dr. Spooner observed in the above, "There exists, I believe, a general consensus of opinion that the modern site of Vaiśāli must be searched for somewhere in Tirhut, the present districts of Muzzaffarpur and Darbhanga, the ancient country of Tirabhukti." pp. 82-83. Dr. Spooner continues; "Mr. Vincent Smith has already shown that the position of Basārh in regard to other places like Patna, etc. fits exactly with the position of Vaiśāli in regard to Pāṭaliputra and similar localities visited by the Chinese....There are moreover, two groups of ruins near Basārh, which correspond with two similar groups, seen by Hieun Tsiang at Vaiśāli, in such a striking way that it would be in vain to search for any other place in Tirhut as a possible site of Vaiśāli."

2 *Hieun Tsiang*, Beal, p. 149. Manu calls it "Giri-Durga."

3 In the first edition, I wrote the *oldest*, for apart from palaeolithic and neolithic implements and certain primitive remains, no monuments were known to exist of an earlier period. "But at a single bound, the modern knowledge of Indian civilisation has been taken back some 3000 years earlier and it has been established that in the third millenium before Christ and even earlier than that the peoples of the Punjab and Sind were living in well-built cities and possessed a relatively mature culture with a high standard of art and craftmanship and a developed system of pictographic writing."

4 Dr. D. B. Spooner. See in this connection, V. H. Jackson, *Notes*

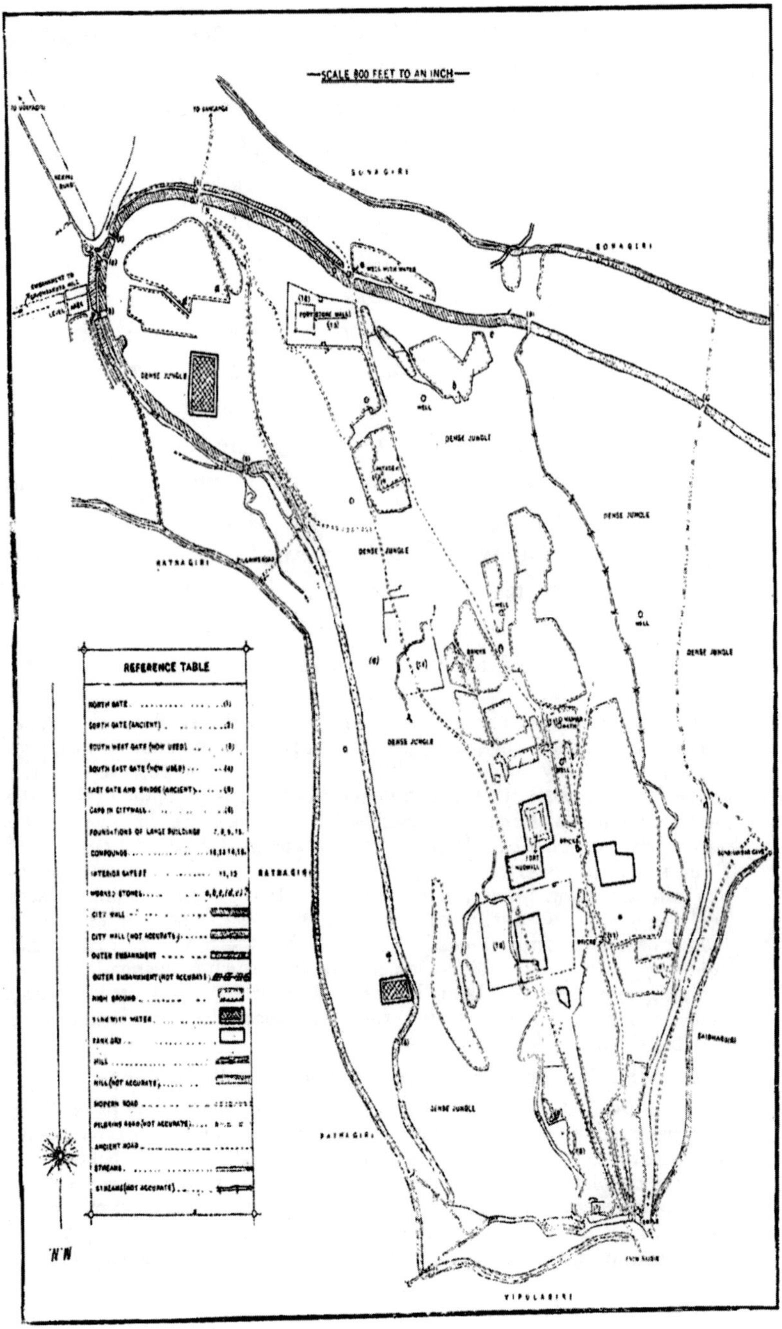

Plan of Old Rajagriha.

Hindu period, while the second name, Rājagṛha came into prominence during the Buddhistic period[1]. Both the names are found in the *Rāmāyaṇa*, but they do not appear to be our capital. Girivraja of the *Rāmāyaṇa* was the capital ef Aśvapati, Bharata's maternal grandfather[2]. The two names are used for the same place and it is described as "city fair", "splendid town", "fair city" ; and from these it is no wonder that the archæologist Cunningham[3] should have mixed up the Girivraja of the *Rāmāyaṇa* with the Girivraja of Magadha, though the city referred to in the former was, undoubtedly, beyond the river Vipāśā in the Punjab, and, as such, could not have any connection with the Girivraja of Magadha. The hero of the Epic, however, had evidently passed through Magadha, as is evidenced by the description of the country given in the *Rāmāyaṇa*.

It was in the days of the *Mahābhārata* that we find enough references to this old historic town, and in its days Girivraja was the capital of Magadha. Before Jarāsandha, the city was perhaps not so strong, for we find Pāṇḍu, the father of the Pāṇḍavas, attacking and killing the king of Magadha in his very capital[4]. Pāṇḍu marched against Dirga, the king of Magadha, who being proud of his strength, had offended many kings. We do not know whether here was any attempt of this king of Magadha at over-lordship, but Pāṇḍu's attacking and killing him in his capital, at any rate, snubbed the ambition of the king of Magadha for over-lordship[5].

---

on old Rajagriha in *A. S. R.*, 1913-14, pp 265-271. Mr. Jackson is undoubtedly the authority on Rājgir.

1 " Rājagṛha was besieged by Khāravela and an army division was inside the Rājagṛha fortress. The king of Magadha moved away to Mathurā during the adverse operation. We do not know the result of the seize." Mr. Jayaswal in *J. B. & O. R. S.*, IV. 368.

2 *Rāmāyaṇa*, LXVIII.

3 *A. S. R.*, I. 20.

4 Ādi, CXIII.

5 *Vide ante* I, f. n. 1, p. 4. Dr. Keith referring to this writes, "It

We also meet with Bṛhadratha[1], a king of Girivraja, who was heroic, proud in battle, mighty, wealthy and matchlessly powerful, and was the best of men, so much so, that he was equal to the "Grandsire" of the Pāṇḍavas. But it was during the days of Jarāsndha, that it became extremely powerful. The description by the panegyrists belonging to the opposite party of Jarāsandha is worth quoting: "The highly powerful, effulgent and persevering Lord Paramount Jarāsandha came to Mathurā, encircled by fourfold ocean-like forces, consisting of war-chariots, containing beautiful seats and drawn by powerful steeds, whose course is never obstructed anywhere, cloud-like elephants embellished with bells and golden seats, ridden by car-warriors well-read in the science of war and driven by clever charioteers, horses going by leaps and bounds, driven by horsemen and resembling clouds and numberless fearful foot-soldiers armed with swords and coats of mail, who could bound up in the sky like serpents."[2] It was quite likely that the first attempt, and at least for sometime quite a successful attempt, to establish *Rājachakravartism*, was made by Jarāsandha, for we see innumerable kings attentively following him and no king was able to equal him in power. As even the Epic, which was the production of his enemies, observes, "Like the sun he robbed all other kings of their splendour and he obtained the sovereignty of the whole world"[3]—a tacit admission of the paramount sovereignty of the king of Magadha. And no wonder that he should have resisted the attempt of Bhīṣma through Yudhisthira to acknowledge Kṛṣṇa as the first one to receive homage, which Jarāsandha claimed to be his own.

Jarāsandha

is certainly possible that the *Chakravarti* doctrine was encouraged by the efforts of some old king of Magadha".

1 Sabhā, XVIII. See also *ante*, p. 3.
2 *Harivaṁśa*, XC.
3 Sabhā, XIX.

The description of the capital of Jarāsandha is also worth mentioning. "The city of the king of Magadha is full of wealth and water. It is very beautiful with trees that stands everywhere in it."[1] And again, "It is full of cattle and other beasts of burden, its stock of water is inexhaustive, it is adorned with fine mansions and it is entirely free from all dangers. The five large hills, Vaibhāra, Varāha, Vṛṣavā, Ṛṣigiri and the beautiful fifth hill Chaityaka,[2] these five hills all with high peaks and with tall trees having cool shades, all being connected with one another, seem jointly to protect the city of Girivraja. The city is impregnable, full of cheerful and well-fed inhabitants, belonging to all the four orders of men. The city is ever enlivened with perennial festivities."[3] And we also find that, "there are many beautiful shops, full of various eatables and garlands, every shop swelling with every article and every kind of wealth that man can desire". Even after the death of Jarāsandha, it retained the vestiges of its ancient glory, for we find Meghasandhi, its king, attacking Arjuna, when he was leading on the sacrificial Aśvamedha horse after the Kurukṣettra War[4].

Description of Girivraja

There is a description of Rājagṛha in the *Rājagṛha Māhātmyam* of the *Vāyu Purāṇa*, where one of the hills itself is called Girivraja, the other four being named Vaibhāra, Vipula, Ratṇākara, and Ratṇāchala[5]. Bathing in the Sarasvatī river at Rājagṛha, according to this *Purāna*, is equivalent to bathing in the Nerbuddā for ten months, and one year in the Ganges. This would

1 *Ibid*, XXII—4.

2 It seems the names of the five hills varied on different occasions. They are now known as Vaibhāra, Vipula, Ratṇagiri, Udayagiri, and Sonāgiri. In the inscriptions on the Jain temples on Mount Vaibhāra, the name is sometimes written Vaibhāra, and sometimes Vyāvahāra.

3 Sabhā, XXI.

4 Aśvamedha, LXXXII, 243-6-3.

5 *Rājagṛha Māhātmyam*, 1. 13.

show the high sanctity which was attached to Rājagṛha by the authors of the Hindu Śāstras.

It was, however, undoubtedly during the Jain and Buddhistic times, especially during the Buddhistic period, that Rājagṛha became more famous. It became a centre of Jainism during the reign of Bimbisāra[1], who is credited with the building of the new Rājagṛha, "the outer town to the north of the ring of hills encircling the ancient fort." It was here that the pathetic incident of Bimbisāra being thrown into prison by his son Ajātaśatru and the heroic attempt of the queen to save her husband happened. Fa-hien, who visiting it about 400 A. D., notes that it was entirely deserted[2], and attributes the building of the new fortified town to king Ajātaśatru, while the other Chinese traveller, Hieun Tsiang, narrates a story about the prevention of fires in Bimbiśāra's capital, Kuśagārapura, which he described as within Rājagṛha, and about the promulgation of a severe law by which the person in whose house a fire was to break out, was to be banished to the "cold forest". As the king's palace was the first to be burnt down, Bimbiśāra, acting up to his own orders, retired to this forest. At this time, the king of Vaiśālī, hearing that Rājā Bimbisāra was dwelling alone in the "cold forest", raised an army and put it in movement to attack him. But the Lords of the Marches, on hearing of it, built a town, and, as the king was the first to hear of it, it was called the royal city of Rājagṛha[3].

There is thus some difference between the two Chinese accounts, though both of them considered "the

---

1 *S. B. E.*, Vol. XIII.

2 Legge, p. 82.

3 In the *Life of Hieun Tsiang* we find that the old city was called Kuśāgārapura, for Magadha then produced some excellent scented grass whence the name was given to the city. p. 113. According to Hardy, *Manual of Buddhism*, it was called Rājagṛha, because not only it was founded by a king, but every house in it resembled a king's house or palace.

ancient city in the valley enclosed by the five Hills", as the "area to be the old city of king Bimbiśara", and "inside it, or at any rate very closely connected with it they saw four stupas commemorating certain incidents in the life of the Buddha"[1], while from the Buddhistic scriptures[2] all that we can gather is that Aājtaśatru strengthened the defences of the old city. Hieun Tsiang's account of the city being built by Bimbisāra is also open to doubt, but here, again, we have to remember the other side of the question, according to which Bimbisāra died in the old city. Further, the *Srāmaṇṇaphalasūtra* says that Ajātaśatru started from the old city to pay his respects to the Buddha, when the King went out to make his confession as a parricide. Sifting these evidences, Principal D. N. Sen, [3]who has made some study of Rājagṛha and its suburbs, basing his opinion on an ancient text came to the conclusion that it was really Ajataśatru who repaired and strengthened the new Rājagṛha and he was not its builder as stated by Dr. Rhys Davids.[4] Mr. K. P. Jayaswal accepts this and says that this adds to our knowledge the fact that the new Rājgir of the Buddhistic Texts, the fort which is in ruins near the Inspection Bungalow at Rājgir really belongs to a period before Ajātaśatru and the Buddha[5]

Importance of Rājagṛha

As we have already observed, it was during the Jain and Buddhistic times that it came into great prominence. Mahāvīra spent considerable time here[6] and is said to

1 *A. S. R.*, 1913-14, *Notes on old Rajagriha* by V. H. Jackson. Cf. Also *A. S R.*, 1905-06.

2 Cf. *Vinaya Piṭakam*, I. 17, 215 and 226. Also *the Digha Nikāya*, II. 76 and 6.

3 *Rajagriha in the Buddhistic Scriptures*, read at the second Oriental Conference at Calcutta.

4 *Buddhist India*, p. 3.

5 *Report of the Second Oriental Conference.* Mr. K. P. Jayaswal accepting this view makes the above observation. This view seems, however, very dubious to Dr. Keith.

6 *S. B. E.*, XXII, 264.

have converted Bimbisāra to Jainism. The eleven *Gaṇadharas*[1] of Mahāvīra died here as being the most sacred of all places. Bimbisāra went to meet the Buddha surrounded by twelve myriads of Brāhmaṇas and householders of Magadha.[2] At Rājagṛha the great Being delivered the *Pabbajjāsutta.*[3] When the Buddha was dwelling at Rājagṛha, in the mountain called the Vulture's Peak, the *Māghasutta* was delivered to the young man Māgha, illustrating the *Dhamma.* When the Bhagavat dwelt at Rājagṛha in *Venuvana*[4] in *Kālāndakanivāpa*, the *Sabhiya Sutta* was delivered to Sabhiya, the Parivrājāka[5]. The great *Mahāparinibbāṇa Sutta* was delivered here on the Vulture's Peak, when Ajātaśatru sent his minister, the Brāhmaṇa Vassakāra, whom we have already met before and whom we shall meet again, to know what the Great One will predict about the king's destroying the Vajjians[6]. No wonder then that the Buddha himself would observe to his favourite attendant Ānanda,[7] "On one occasion Ānanda, I was dwelling at that same Rājagaha in the Banyan Grove, on one occasion at the same Rājagaha at the Robber's Cliff, on one occasion at that same Rājagaha in the Sattapaṇṇi Cave on the slope of Mount Vebhāra, on one occasion at that same Rājagaha at that Black Rock on the slope of Mount Isigili, on one occasion at that same Rājagaha in the Tapoda Grove,[8] on one occasion at that same Rājagaha in the Bamboo grove in the Squirrel's Feeding Ground, on one occasion

1 *Ibid*, XIII, 287.
2 *Ibid*, XIII, 136.
3 *Ibid*, X, (ii) 67.
4 *Ibid*, (ii) 80.
5 *Ibid*, 85.
6 *Ibid*, XI, ii ff.
7 *Ibid*, XI, 56
8 *Saṁyūtha-Nikāvaka*, I, 8 ff.

at that same Rājagaha in Jīvaka's[1] Mango Grove, on one occasion at the same Rājagaha in the Deer Forest of *Maddakuthi* and all these, as the Tathāgata expressed are pleasant".[3] Indeed, many a corner of Rājagṛha is associated with the Buddha's name. It was at this place that he had first begged for his alms, when king Bimbisāra feeling interested in Siddhārtha, tried to tempt him with wealth and make him share his kingdom with him; here[4], he spent considerable time on the Vulture's Peak in the *Venuvana* in *Kālāndakanivāpa*. It was here that[5] Ajātaśatru met the Buddha, who delivered a large number of his discourses. After Buddha's death the first Buddhist Council was held here. And it is, therefore, no wonder that time after time we should hear of Rājagṛha in the Buddhistic scriptures, as "the great city", "rich", "happy", "thriving", "as the royal city with[6] its beautiful palaces". It was considered fit by Ānanda[7] to be one of the few cities where the Buddha could attain *Nirvāna.*

Long after the *Nirvāna* of the Buddha, well might Aśvaghoṣa speak of the city in high terms as distinguished by its encircling hills, well guarded by and adorned with mountains, and consecrated and hallowed by auspicious and sacred places, like a "Brāhmaṇa amidst a holy calm going to the uppermost heaven[8]." The *Vimāna Vatthu*[9] speaks of it as the best of towns well-measured

1 For an account relating to Jīvaka, vide *Vinaya Piṭaka*, I. 286 ff.

2 Vide *J. B. & O. R. S.*, Vol. IV, *Sites in Rajgir connected with Buddha's name and his Disciples* by Mr. D. N. Sen.

3 *S. B. E.*, X(ii) 67.

4 *Ibid*, X (ii) 85.

5 *Dialogues of the Buddha.*

6 *Meditations on Buddha Amitābha.*

7 *Suttakritāṅga.*

8 *Buddha-charita*

9 I. 16.

between the hills, while its commentary refers to the fact of "this best of towns" being built by Mahāgovinda Paṇḍita versed in the science of town-planning.

Fa-hien has not much to say of Rājagṛha, while, though Hieun Tsiang takes up a cosiderable room, he refers only to the destruction of the outer walls where no remnants had been left, though the inner walls which were in a ruined state were in existence[1]. With the removal of the capital to Pāṭaliputra all its glories vanished. Its condition is even now deplorable, and thorough excavations are needed. "The place has been occupied at different times by Mussalmans and Brāhmaṇas, by whom the Buddhist *stupas* and vihārs were pulled down to furnish materials for tombs, masjids and temples. All the eminences that once must have been crowned with objects of Buddhist worship are now covered with graves and all the Brāhmanical temples about the hotsprings have been constructed with the large bricks of Buddhist *stupas*"[2]. Such is the present sad condition of the great old historic town.

Pāṭaliputra

Pāṭaliputra arose after Girivraja. We have already mentioned that Rājagṛha was considered fit for the *Nirvāṇa* of the Buddha, but Pāṭaliputra was not reckoned by Ānanda as sufficiently important to witness the scene of the great event—it was *not* a *Mahānagara* then. This shows that Pāṭaliputra was at that time considered to be of less importance than Rājagṛha. The *Mahāparinibbanā Sutta* refers to the fact that the great Buddha, after proceeding from Rājagṛha (which he remembered just before his *Parinibbāṇa* as "delightful") through Nālandā, suggested to his favourite disciple that they should go to Pāṭaligāma[3]. As usual, Ānanda consented, and accompanied by a large body of disciples, they

1 Beal, *Buddhist Records of the Western World*, II. 165.

2 *A. S. R.*, I.24.

3 *Dīgha Nikāya*, II, 4.89.

reached it, and here they were very hospitably received[1]. The blessed one, next day, getting up at early dawn, addressed the venerable Ānanda thus: "Who is it Ānanda, that is laying out a city at Pāṭaligāma?" Ānanda replied, "Sunīdha and Vassakāra, O Lord, the chief ministers of Magadha, are laying out a city at Pāṭaligāma to keep back the Vajjis". On hearing this the Great One said, "Here, Ānanda! I see with divine and clear vision, surpassing that of men, Gods[2] in many thousands, taking up their residence at Pāṭaligāma. As far, O Ānanda, as there are noble places of residence, as far as merchants travel, this will become the chief town, the Pāṭaliputra, a centre for the interchange of all kinds of ware[3]." And the blessed one also foretold, "of Pāṭaliputra[4], O Ānanda! there will be three sources of danger, either from fire, or from water[5], or from internal dissension". We are then told that the great one left the village "by the western gate"[6]; then turning northward, he passed the Ganges at a ferry; and these were called Gotama's gate and Gotama's ferry[7].

---

1 Cf. also Bigandet's *Life of Gautama.*

2 Or "many fairies".

3 Rockhill's *Life of Buddha*, p. 125.

4 The first authentic references to Pāṭaliputra of which the date can be fixed with certainty are in Asoka's Girnar Rock Edict and in his Sārnath Pillar Edict.

5 It is interesting to refer to Dr. Spooner's *Report on the Excavations at Pāṭaliputra* which prove two of these assertions made by the Buddha. *J. R. A. S.*, 1915.

6 Hieun Tsiang says, "In the old time, Tathāgata, being about to attain *Nirvāṇa* was going northward to Kusinārā, when turning round to the south and looking back at Magadha he stood upon this stone and referred to the building of the Capital at Pāṭaliputra" (*Beal, II.* 90).

7 *Māhāparinibbāṇa Sutta, S. B. E.*, XI. 21. This event happened according to Mr. Jayaswal in 544 or 545 *B. C.*, *J. B. & O. R. S.*, *V.* Dr. Keith, however, is not prepared to accept this date. "The efforts to rehabilitate the old date 544 B. C. for the *Nirvāṇa* are certainly unsatisfactory." He goes on, "they contradict, *inter alia*, the plain fact that the Buddhist scriptures recognise that the Buddha [illegible] Mahāvīra who certainly was alive after 544 B. C."

And because it was associated with the Buddha's blessing that half of the remains of Ānanda were taken possession of by Ajātaśatru who built a chaitya over it[1]. Then come the achievements of Udayin, to whom both the Brāhmaṇas[2] and Jains attribute the foundation of Kusumapura on the south bank of the Ganges, the new city, which was either indentical with the later Pāṭaliputra, or in the immediate neighbourhood was built the fortress, which Ajātaśatru had established at the village of Pāṭal, as a protection against the Vajjian confederacy.

The Jain accounts are available in Hem Chandra's *Pāriśiṣṭaparvan.* This author tells us that Udaya, who ascended the throne after his father's death, was overwhelmed with grief, and was altogether unable to attend to the affairs of the state. His ministers, therefore, advised him to bid good-bye to the scenes associated with his late father, to build up a new city. Experts versed in reading signs and portents[3] were ordered to find out a suitable spot which they did on the bank of the Ganges where they found a Pāṭali tree shining red with its glorious burden of flowers, with a thick foliage, and casting a shadow over an extensive region like a canopy over the earth, while the whole place appeared to them to be full of promising signs. This spot was approved by the king[4]. We then get an account of the

1 Rockhill'e *Life of Buddha.*

2 Cf. *Brahmāṇda Purāṇa, Upodghata pada*, 116. From a drama of Bhāsa, *Pratijñā Yaugandharāyana*, it appears that Darśaka gave his sister in marriage to the king of the Vatsya country to hold in check a confederacy of kings (probably of north Bihar) in order to watch these enemies more effectively and also to take advantage of the river highway for the commerce which was fast increasing. Owing to the intercourse with the west, Pāṭaliputra was selected as the Capital.

3 Here was traced the skull of a famous Jaina saint. The artisans of the king, arriving at the spot, went round the tree in an ever-widening circle, till they heard the cry of a jackal. There they dropped the measuring thread.

4 According to M. M. H. P. Sāstri, the transfer was within two generations after the Buddha's death. If the Buddha died in 543 B.C.

building of the town. The architects measured their lines from the point where the Pāṭali tree was, and keeping it to the east, they proceeded towards the west and then towards the north, thus forming the western boundary; and next towards the east, marking the northern limits; and again towards the south, finally coming back to the Pāṭali tree, from which the town acquired the name of Pāṭaliputra, and which was adorned with palaces, marts, hospitals and the other requisites of a capital town.

The above is, of course, a traditionary account, but it is also supported by the Purāṇas[1], where we find that king Udaya "will establish in the fourth year of his reign, a city called Kusumapura[2] on the southern bank of the Ganges." At any rate, it can be said with almost perfect certainty that Pāṭaliputra succeeded Rājagṛha as the capital of Magadha, and that event took place shortly after the death of the Buddha.

So far as the name is concerned, Hieun Tsiang gives us a story[3], which has been interpreted in various ways. Once on a time, a very learned Brāhmaṇa had a

---

the transfer according to Mr. Sāstri must have taken place about 500 B. C.; if in 483 B. C., the transfer took place about 410 B. C. The fact that the place was a village and an unfortified one at the time of the Buddha's going to Kuśinārā, as compared with the description of Megasthenes that it was one of the largest and most prosperous as well as fortified towns of India, show that some considerable time must have elapsed between the two.

1 *Vāyu*, 99 and *Brahmānda*, 2.

2 *Mudrārākṣasa* tells us that Kusumapura was another name of Pāṭaliputra.

3 In *Hieun Tsiang's Life* we find, "In old days, when men's lives were of immeasurable strength, this town was called, Kusumapura, because the king's palace had so many flowers and it was called so. Afterwards, when men's minds dwindled down to a few thousand years, then it was called Pāṭaliputra after the pāṭali tree." (Beal, II. p. 101). The same traveller observes, "when the old capital of Kusumapura was changed, this town was chosen, and from the circumstance of the genii building the mansion of the youth the name henceforth of the country was Pāṭaliputra". (*Records of the Western World*, II. 85). Beal observes, "From this it would appear that Kusumapura was not

large number of disciples. A party of these on a certain occasion, wandered in the woods, and a young man of their number appeared unhappy and disconsolate. To cheer and amuse the gloomy youth, his companions agreed to get up a mock marriage for him. A man and a woman were chosen to act as parents for the bridegroom, aud another couple represented the parents of the imaginary bride. They were all near a Pāṭali tree at the time, and as the name of the tree had a feminine termination they decided to make it a bride. When all was over, the other youngmen wanted their companion, the bridegroom, to go with them, but he insisted on remaining near the tree. Here, at dusk, an old man appeared with his wife and a young maiden, and the old man gave the maiden to the young student to be his wife. The couple lived together for a year, when a son was born to them. The student, now tired of the lovely wild life of the woods, wanted to go back to his home, but the old man, his father-in-law, induced him to stay on, by the promise of a properly-built establishment ; and the promise was carried out very promptly. Afterwards when the seat of Government was removed to this place, it got the name of Pāṭaliputra, because it had been built by the gods for the son of the Pāṭali-tree, and it has kept the name ever since"[1].

---

at the same site as Pāṭaliputra. Rājagṛha was the capital in the time of Ajātaśatru and it was he who strengthened Pāṭaliputra. In the next clause it is said that Asoka changed his capital from Rājagṛha to Pāṭaliputra. He is described as the great grandson of Bimbisāra and therefore grandson of Ajātaśatru. The *Vāyu Purāṇa* states that Kusumapura or Pāṭaliputra was founded by Rājā Udayāśva, the grandson of Ajātaśatru, but the *Mahāvaṁśa* makes Udaya the son of the king" (II. 84).

1 Mr. Watters adds the following note : 'The place where the mock ceremony took place was close to a pātali, Bignonia suaveolens or Trumpet-flower tree, and the bride was called Miss Pātali, her father in the play giving a branch of the tree, as his daughter, to the student to be his wife. Afterwards as the story shows, the Dryads of the tree, like the melancholy mortal, took the whole affair in earnest and made the marriage a reality. The old man and the old mother and her

CAPITAL DISCOVERED AT PATALIPUTRA (AND CONSIDERED TO BE "QUASI—PERSEPOLITAN")

To face p. 54.

STONE-RAILING FROM PATALIPUTRA

To face p. 54.

Leaving aside the legendary account, we first get a historical account of the city from Megasthenes, the ambassador of the Greek king Selukos Nikator, who came to Pāṭaliputra in or about 303 B. C., and who has given us a good account of Pālimbothra. It is needless for me to go into any details about the description of the Capital situated then at the confluence of the Ganges and the Son, eighty stadia in length and fifteen in breadth, of the size of a parallelogram, wlth its pallisades and a ditch six hundred feet in breadth and thirty cubits in depth, and a wall with its tower. We can ignore the confusion of Megasthenes regarding the Brāhmaṇas, and S'ramaṇas, his mistakes about the seven castes of the people, though his "seven classes may truly reflect the various activities which a Greek resident at Pāṭaliputra could see going on round about him in the third century B. C."[1]. We are inclined to regret his sad omission of anything regarding the languages of India. We cannot, however, pass by the account of the administration of the capital with its thirty Municipal Commissioners and six Boards and its census ; and we cannot but feel proud of the high compliments he pays our ancestors about their honesty. Also, we cannot but refer to the fact that the description of the court and civil and military administration, as given by him has been amply corroborated[2] by the discovery of the *Arthaśāstra* of Chāṇakya, and we cannot but acknowledge our great indebtedness to Dr. R. Shamasāstry of Mysore in this connection. And though, as Mr. Vincent Smith has well observed: "It is not desirable to amalgamate the

daughter are the god and the goddesses of the tree, and the daughter becomes the student's wife. When he proposes to go away, the old god by his superhuman agency builds for the residence of his newly-born grandson, a substantial establishment. This was the nucleus of the city which from the story of its origin obtained and kept the name of Pāṭaliputra". II. 88.

1 *The Cambridge History of India*, I. 409.

2 Cf. V. A. Smith, *The Early History of India*, p. 144.

rules laid down in the *Arthaśāstra* with the descriptions recorded by the Greeks, because the latter present to us the impressions made upon foreign observers of institutions actually existing at a particular date, 300 B. C., in round numbers, after the foundation of the Maurya Empire; whereas the former expresses the arrangements favoured by Brāhmaṇa ministers, as suitable for any independent kingdom at any time,"[1] there can be no denying the fact that its discovery has widened the path of scholars interested in ancient Indian culture and we can certainly take credit for the fact that its author, Kauṭilya, had his school of politics here, the same Kauṭilya who established Chandragupta on the throne of Magadha.

I have quoted an English historian saying that the Greek account has been amply corroborated by the *Arthaśāstra.* I would go still further and say that in many matters the two accounts tally wonderfully. Let us first put before you the account of Megasthenes regarding the administration of Pāṭaliputra, the capital and then take up each point one by one and place side by side that of Chāṇakya, and I will leave it to you to say whether there is really a very great difference. I am quoting and comparing both at some length.

Megasthenes observes: "Of the great officers of state, some have charge of the market, others of the city, others of the soldiers. Some superintend the rivers (canals) measuring the land as is done in Egypt, and inspect the sluices by which water is let out from the canals into their branches, so that every one may have an equal share of it.

"The same persons have charge also of the huntsmen (surely only the royal huntsmen) and are entrusted

1 *The Early History of India*, p. 145, "We may accept it as an authoritative account of political & social conditions in the Gangetic plain in the age of Alexander the Great, 325 B. C." This view, as I have observed in several places, has not been universally accepted.

with the power of rewarding or punishing them according to their deserts.[1]

"They collect the taxes, and superintend the occupations connected with land (that is no doubt look after the royal dues arising out of them) as those of woodcutters, carpenters, blacksmiths and miners. They construct roads and, at every ten stadia, set up a pillar to show the byroads and distances.

"Those who have charge of the city are divided into six bodies of five each. The members of the first look after everything related to the industrial arts.

"Those of the second look after the entertainment of foreigners. To these they assign lodgings; and they keep watch over their modes of life by means of those persons whom they give to them as servants. They escort them on the way, when they leave the country, or, in the event of their dying, they forward

1 Among others, Dr. Keith is strongly of opinion that the *Artha-śāstra* was not the work of Kauṭilya, minister of Chandragupta. He says, "It must remain an open question whether in the treatise are preserved any authentic remains of his views, if we accept tradition and believe that he actually existed as an important political factor. The evidence in favor of an affirmative reply in this matter are unfortunately far from strong; what does appear to be the fact is that probably, especially under the Gupta dynasty with the revival of Hinduism the fame of the minister of the ancient Chandragupta evoked the production of maxims ascribed to him. But at any rate, the *Arthaśāstra* should no longer be used as a *prima facie* authority for the period 300 B. C. In a letter to me he writes, "Stein who in his *Megasthenes Und Kauṭilya* has compared the various items minutely, has found nothing noteworthy in support of the practical contemporaneity of the two accounts and Jolly has adduced a great deal of evidence in the opposite sense, while many years ago, in the *J. R. A. S.*, 1916, pp. 130-7, I opposed the current theory of the authencity of Kauṭilya. There is of course, no reason, not to use Kauṭilya as throwing light on Asoka, but I should certainly not do so, on the theory that it existed before Asoka borrowed his statecraft from it. Its value is that it represents a great deal of traditional statecraft, not that it is the work of the minister of Chandragupta." Dr Jolly is equally convinced that if "there was a minister Chāṇakya of Chandragupta at all, he was not the author of the *Arthaśāstra*, nor does it express his views, but it is rather a product of the 4th century A. D. Dr. Winternitz also rejects Chāṇakya's authorship (*Calcutta Review*, 1924.) and leaves it to the 3rd century A. D. But both Drs. Shāmasāstry & the late Ganapati Sāstri have no doubts as to the author. Vide also *the Calcutta Review*, XII, 512 ff, and XIII, 288 ff,

their property to their relatives. They take care of them when they are sick, and if they die, bury them.

"The third body consists of those who inquire when and how births and deaths occur, with a view not only to levy a tax, but also in order that births and deaths among the high and the low may not escape the cognisance of Government.

Megasthenes

"The fourth class superintends trade and commerce. Its members have charge of weights and measures, and see that the products, in their season, are sold by public notice. No one is allowed to deal in more than one kind of commodity unless he pays a double tax.

"The fifth class supervises manufactured articles, which they sell by public notice. What is new is sold separately from what is old; there is a fine for mixing the two together.

"The sixth and last class consists of those who collect the tenths of the prices of the articles sold. Fraud in the payment of this tax is punished with death".

I have inflicted upon you a long extract, but now I will put before you the passages from the *Arthaśāstra*, one by one, comparing the two.

Megasthenes speaks of the great officers of state, and in the *Arthaśāstra* we have the Collector-General who attended to the construction of the treasury house, trading house, the store-house of grains, the store-house of forest produce, the armoury and the jail[1]. The other great officers mentioned by Chāṇakya[2] are the Superintendents of Gold, Store-house, Commerce, Forest-produce, Armoury, Weights and Measures, Tolls, Weaving, Agriculture, Liquors, Slaughter-houses, Ships, Cows,

---

and 466, where Dr. Narendranath Law firmly maintains the authencity of the work. Vide also Dr. R. K. Mookerjee's Introduction to N. Law's *Ancient Indian Polity*.

1 II. VI. The market of Megasthenes figures in the *Arthaśāstra* as *Paṇyapattaṇa* (II. 1.)

2 Book II.

and Horses, Elephants, Chariots, Infantry, Passports, Pasture lands, and the Superintendent of the City. It is not possible for me here to discuss the duties of each officer, the very names of whom would indicate to a great extent their respective duties, many of them being indicated by Megasthenes.

Megasthenes and Kauṭilya

The Greek writer makes mention of the officer in charge of the city, and we have the *Nāgaraka*[1], the officer in charge of the capital city, who was to look after the affairs of the capital. And we have also a *Gopa* and a *Sthānika*[2]. We have in the former book the officer in charge of the soldiers and in the latter work the Superintendent of Chariots, the Superintendent of Infantry, and the Commander-in-chief placed over the whole army—*Chaturaṅgabala*, *i. e.*, elephants, horses, chariots and infantry. The former speaks of the Superintendent of the canals, measuring the sluices, while the latter refers to the punishment of persons who obstructed or did any kind of mischief to these sluice-gates[3].

Regarding the hunters mentioned by Megasthenes and their duties, we have references in the other account also, *e. g.* in Book II, Chapters I and XXXIV, where the duties of the hunters are given. Taxes were collected from various sources, and the Collector-General[4] was to attend to the collection of revenue from forts, country-parts, mines, buildings, gardens, forests, herds of cattle, and roads of traffic.

So far as occupations connected with land were concerned, and Megasthenes refers to the looking after the royal dues arising after them, we have the Superinten-

---

1 *The Arthaśāstra*, Book II, Chap. XXXVI.

2 Looking after one quarter of the Capital as in p. 181, English edition.

3 III. 1 & 10.

4 II. 6.

dent of Agriculture[1]. We will discuss the question regarding the royal dues in one of our subsequent lectures but perhaps it would not be altogether out of place just to mention how Chāṇakya enjoined that the king was to protect agriculture[2] from the molestation of oppressive fines, free labour and taxes. Megasthenes mentions the occupations of carpenters and blacksmiths in connection with the officer whose duty it was to superintend the occupations connected with land; and the names of these two classes of workmen occur also in the *Artha-śāstra*, when its author speaks of the duties of the Superintendent of Agriculture and insists that agricultural labourers shall not in any way be deprived of the assistance of blacksmiths and carpenters[3]. Chāṇakya attaches great importance to mining and those who were connected with it, *viz.*, the miners, who are also mentioned by Megasthenes. There was the Superintendent of Mines,[4] who was required to have a knowledge of metallurgy, and the art of distillation and condensation of mercury, and the methods of testing gems. He had as his assistants, experts in mineralogy, while he had under him labourers who were well-equipped to work in mines with necessary implements[5]. Before the discovery of Kauṭilya's *Arthaśātra*, we had to depend on Megasthenes for reference to numerous ores of metals underground, containing "much gold and silver and copper and iron in no small quantity, and even tin and other metals";[6] but now after the discovery of this invaluable treatise, we can have any amount of details regarding the importance given to mining.

Magasthenes and Kauṭilya

1 II. 24.
2 II. 1.
3 II. 1.
4 II. 12.
5 Vide *Lectures on the Economic Condition of Ancient India*, p. 108.
6 Megasthenes, I. 1.

Megasthenes, in his account, refers to the construction of roads, and Chāṇakya also lays stress on it[1]. There is one difference, however, between the two, for while Megasthenes refers to the placing of a pillar at every ten stadia, Chāṇakya does not seem to refer to it, though he gives minute directions regarding the width of the various roads[2]. But we have to remember that the whole of the *Arthaśāstra* has not yet been discovered and many passages have not been properly interpreted.

Megasthenes and Kauṭilya

The Grecian ambassador of Selukos refers to the members of the first board of Pātaliputra looking after the industrial arts and speaks of the fourth class as consisting of the artisans.[3] Indeed, the references in Megasthenes, Strabo[4], and Arrian[5], go to prove that industries were well-organised and well-looked after. We have also in the *Arthaśāstra* that "those who conspire to lower the quality of the works of artisans, to hinder their income or purchase shall be heavily fined".[6]

Regarding the attention to foreigners as testified to by Megasthenes, we find in Chāṇakya that the Superintendent of Commerce was to show favour to foreigners[7]; while, if the interpretation be correct, the Superintendent of Ships[8] was to show all possible concern for weather-beaten ships, while the Superintendent of Commerce was to show favour to those who imported foreign merchandise.

In the next paragraph. Megasthenes speaks of the registration of births and deaths. The Census referred

1 II. 1.
2 II. 4.
3 P. 42 of McCrindle's edition.
4 *Ibid*, P. 54.
5 *Ibid*, P. 211.
6 IV. 2.
7 II. 16.
8 II. 28.

to here, I shall discuss at length in a subsequent lecture, and I need not, therefore, dilate on it in this place. As Mr. Vincent Smith[2] has observed rightly, "Even the Anglo-Indian administration with its complex organisation and European notions of the value of statistical information, did not attempt the collection of vital statistics until very recent times, and has always experienced great difficulty in securing reasonable accuracy in the figures".

Megasthenes and Kauṭilya

The fourth Board of Megasthenes refers to those officers whose duty it was to superintend trade and commerce. We have in the *Arthaśāstra* a reference to the Superintendent of Commerce[3] who had various duties to perform, one of which, viz., showing favour to those who imported foreign merchandise, we have already referred to. Perhaps his most important duty was to prevent, what we would call now-a-days, *cornering*[4].

The officer belonging to the same Board, who concerned himself with weights and measures, finds his place as the Superintendent of weights and measures in Chāṇakya[5]. Very likely the Superintendent of Commerce performed this duty also[6], and the regulations were so strict that even the slightest difference in weights and measures was severely dealt with. Sale by public notice, as referred to by Megasthenes, finds a place in the *Arthaśāstra*, where we are told that, "the merchandise being placed near the flag of the toll-house, the merchants shall declare its quantity and price, and cry out thrice, 'who will purchase such a quantity of merchandise for so much price.' ?[7]

---

1 II. 16
2 *The Early History of India*, p. 128.
3 II. 16.
4 Vide *Lectures on the Economic Condition of Ancient India*, p.125.
5 II. 19.
6 IV. 2.
7 II. 21.

Wooden Platforms in Mauryan Palace—Front View.
(Tata Excavations at Pataliputra)

The Same—Side View.

Megasthenes and Kauṭilya

Referring to manufactured articles, Megasthenes says that "what is new is sold separately from what is old", an order promulgated by Chāṇakya being to the effect that "old collection shall be replaced by new supply."[1] In another place[2] he lays down that "the sale or mortgage of articles as superior, though they are really inferior" was to be heavily punished.

The last class of officers referred to by Megasthenes was they who collected a tenth of the prices af articles sold and represented the Superintendent of Tolls[3] of the *Arthaśāstra* who collected his dues on all merchandise[4], although the rates of toll varied for different commodities, and were fixed in accordance with the customs of countries, or of communities, either old or new[5].

I hope you will now allow me to reiterate that in many respects the two accounts, those of Chāṇakya and Megasthenes, tally well, and we cannot but regret that a large portion of the work of Megasthenes has been lost, for if the mere fragments that survive in quotations by later authors give us such a wonderful account of our old city and its administration, what might not have we expected had the whole work been extant? The discovery of the *Arthaśāstra* has proved to the world that Megasthenes did not write merely mendacious stories, and there is now little doubt regarding his accounts[6].

The next references we get of Pāṭaliputra are in the fifth Rock Edict and in the Sārnath Edict, of Asoka in both of which the name of the capital is distinctly mentioned; and it was under the direct patronage of Asoka and at Pāṭaliputra that the Buddhist council was held,

1 II. 15.
2 IV. 11.
3 II. 21.
4 II. 22.
5 *Ibid.*
6 I need not refer here, to the excavations of Pāṭaliputra for which vide *J. R. A. S.*, 1915, Dr. Spooner's *The Zoroastrian Period of Indian History*, pp. 63 and 405, and *ibid.*p. 800. Also, *ibid.* 1916, 138.

and it was at this time that Tissa Moggaliputra composed the latest book on the three Piṭakas living in the court of Asoka, here at Pāṭaliputra.

Pāṭaliputra continued to be the capital during the Suṅga dynasty when Puṣyamitra, the founder of the dynasty signalised the renaissance of Hinduism by his *Aśvamedha* sacrifice. Not only was this a revival of Brhāmaṇism, but very likely here was another attempt to establish the authority of a paramount sovereign in Northern India. It was during the reign of this Puṣyamitra that occurred the invasion of Menander, who even threatened Pāṭaliputra, the capital[2], but he was repulsed. Patañjali the grammarian, flourished here at this time and was a contemporary of Puṣyamitra whose Horse-Sacrifice is recorded by him. At that time Pāṭaliputra was a great city along the banks of the Son. Its walls and palaces were massive and there were guides to Pāṭaliputra, while there were roads from it, branching off in all directions.

Pāṭaliputra, after this, lost much of its importance, and Mr. Vincent Smith's assertion that "the imperial city of Pāṭaliputra is known to have continued to be a place of importance as late as the fifth century "[3] is not supported by facts. Neither can his statement that, "the high importance attached by the founder of the Gupta era in A. D. 320 to his alliance with a Lichchhavi princess suggests that during the third century Pāṭaliputra may have been held by the non-Aryan Lichchhavis of Vaiśālī"[4], go unchallenged. As we have already discussed this question in the beginning of this lecture, we need not revert to it here. It is, of course, true that Chandra Gupta, the first of the Gupta kings, again made Pāṭaliputra important, though soon after it

1 *The Early History of India*, p. 227.
2 *Ibid*, p. 228.
3 *Ibid*, p. 296.
4 *The Early History of India*, p. 296.

General View of Excavations at Pataliputra.
(showing rows of polished Sandstone Fragments)

Polished Sandstone Column.
(Tata Excavations at Pataliputra)

To face p. 64.

Excavations at Pataliputra—Gupta Remains.

The Same:

ceased to be the ordinary residence of the Gupta sovereigns. From this time to the time of the advent of the Pāla Kings, Pāṭaliputra ceased to be an important place ; and in the description of Fa-hien, the Chinese traveller, we have only a reminiscence of its lost glories ; for there were only the ruins, though the walls, doorways and the sculptured designs were no human work[1]. And Hieun Tsiang's account also is in the same melancholy strain. When he came here in the seventh century, the city was deserted, only the foundation-walls surviving. The chinese writer Ma-twan-lin says that, in 756, a portion of the town was destroyed through erosion by the river Son.

Long, long after, in the reign of Dharmapāla, Pāṭaliputra again rose to prominence, and as mentioned before,[2] this powerful king issued one of his grants from Pāṭaliputra which is described as his *Jayaskanadhābára*, *i. e.*, royal camp[3]. In the Monghyr *Praśasti*[4] of Devapāla, there is also a reference to the *Paramasaugata Parameśvara Paramabhattāraka Mahārājā S'rī* Dharmapāla, and there is mentioned the name of a town as S'rīnagara which has been identified with Pāṭaliputra.[5] And I may here as well record some more epigraphic references to it.

(1) In the tenth century A. D., a Pāṭaliputra Brāhmaṇa was considered as the most suitable for receiving gifts and was given more than four hundred villages[6].

(2) In the Bongāvon plate of Govinda Chandra and his queen, it is recorded that the king *Paramabhattáraka Mahārāj adhirāja Para-*

1 Fa-hien, chap, XXVII.
2 *Vide, ante*, p. 32.
3 *Epigraphia Indica*, IV.
4 *Indian Antiquary*, XXI.
5 *Vide, ante*, p. 33.
6 *Epigraphia Indica*, *IX*, p. 40.

meśvara Govinda Chandra Deva, and his queen the *Paṭṭamahādevi* Mahārājñi Gosaladevi, endowed with all royal prerogatives after having bathed in the Ganges settled a village on a student who had come from Pāṭaliputra[1].

(3) In the Nālandā Copper-Plate discovered by Pandita Hirananda Sastri, there is also the mention of Śrīnagara which has been identified with Pāṭaliputra.

(4) The Srāvaṇa Belgola Epitaph of Narasiṃha shows that even in the 12th century, Pāṭaliputra was considered as the most important place for learned disputations[3].

This is some of the epigraphic evidence we have. But Pāṭaliputra had lost its glories, and there was no king here, no court, no pomp. It remained in this condition for ages and ages, till the creation of the ROYAL province of Bihar again has made it resume its old position to a certain extent. Whether it should ever be able to emulate its old glories, is what more than any mortal can foretell[4].

---

1 *Ibid* V. Keilhorn, *Northern List*, Nos. 127 & 131. King Govinda had also a Buddhist Queen *E. I.*, IX., 321.

2 This was discovered by Hirananda Sastri M.A., M.O.L., at Nālandā during the course of his archaeological exploration in 1921. The introductory portion of the inscription, consisting of the first twenty-five lines, is identical with the similar portion of the Munghir copper-plate grant of the same king (*Indian Antiquary*, XXI, pp. 253-258). The inscription is written in early Devanāgri Script and its language is Sanskrit. A seal is soldered to the plate and bears the legend Sri-Devapāladevasya, meaning of the illustrious Davapāladeva, written below the emblem of the *dharmachakra* placed between two gazelles as in the seals of other Pāla kings (*Epigraphia Indica*, XVII). "The way in which this record speaks of Nālandā, would show that it continued to be as important a centre of Buddhist lore as it was during the time of Hieun Tsiang's visit." *Ibid*, p 13.

3 *E. I.*, V. 151.

4 The discovery of the image, known as the Didārganj image, five miles east of Patna City and first brought to light by the author of this book, may be mentioned here in passing, as it has excited great interest throughout the cultural world. The image is certainly one of the glories of Magadha.

The Didarganj Image.

APPENDIX

It would not be uninteresting to refer here to an account of Pāṭaliputra as given in an old Hindi manuscript. In the *Satya Yuga* (the Golden age) there lived, in a city called Kosambi, a certain Brāhmaṇa whose name was Bhumideva. He had two sons, Kuśa and Bikuśa, married respectively to Pramati and Sumati, daughters of a great Muni (sage) named Sarvasiddhi. It once happened that Kuśa and Bikuśa were reduced to great difficulties, and in order to recover themselves, they determined to try their fortunes abroad and they left home accompanied by their wives. After a few days' journey, on a certain night, the two brothers left their wives asleep in a jungle and went away. Soon after the helpless ladies awoke and began to lament. Meanwhile, Pārvati and Mahādeva passed by that way, and the former requested Mahādeva to take pity on the poor women, and was told that that very night Sumati would give birth to a son, who should be named Putra and as often as he would awake from sleep a thousand gold *mohurs* would fall from his head. During the night this prophecy was fulfilled, and as the child awoke from his first sleep a thousand gold *mohurs* fell from his head. The women suspected that the money was left there by some thief, and lest they should be caught and punished as guilty, they thought it advisable to leave that place. But to their great surprise wherever they went, the same miracle was repeated. They at last discovered the secret and came to Benares and settled there. Putra soon became very rich. His charity knew no bounds, and from every part of the world men came to share his gifts. Kuśa and Bikuśa were now living in Karnāta, begging from door to door. When they heard of the benevolence of Putra, they came to Benares to receive alms at his hands. As the two brothers were standing at the gate of Putra's palace, Sumati, who was walking on the upper verandah of her mansion, saw and recognised them. They were admitted into the house and treated with great respect: Kuśa and Bikuśa now began to live happily. When Putra was sixteen years old, his father became jealous of him and engaged some *chandāls* to murder him. The *chandāls* came to the innocent boy and told him that they were the *Pāndās* (votaries) of the goddess Vindhya-Vāsini, and were sent to take him to that goddess to fulfil certain vows that were made for his sake when he was in his mother's womb. The father, too, supported this statement, and poor Putra was snatched away from his home, accompanied by a single attendant. When the *chandāls* arrived at the middle of a huge jungle, they told the whole truth to the boy, but whenever they attempted to put him to death, their swords fell off their hands. At last the villains promised to save the boy, on receipt of a large sum of money. This being done, the *chandāls* returned to Kāsi and informed Bikuśa that what he had ordered was done and obtained a rich prize.

The boy, left alone in the midst of the dreadful wood, did not know what to do. Night came on and he ascended a tree. In the meantime, two *Rākṣasas*, Sankaṭa and Bikaṭa, came and promising that no injury need be feared from them requested him to decide a case. They said, "We are the sons of a great *Rākṣasa* named Karibaka. Our father once satisfied Mahādeva and obtained three things from him. The first was a pair of shoes by means of which a man can travel thousands of miles in a moment ; the second was a bag from which all sorts of jewels may be extracted whenever the hand is put into it, and the third a rod, which, if turned round, will in a short space of time create a large and magnificent city. Now our father is dead and it is to be decided who should own these." Putra pointed out a large garden and said, "Go to that garden, leaving these things here, and whosoever returns first from that place becomes the owner of these things." The brothers ran towards the garden. In the meantime, a voice from heaven told Putra that he was destined to become a great man and he should wear the pair of shoes and fly at once to Siṃhaladvīpa, with the bag and the rod. The boy followed the advice, and in a moment he was on the banks of a beautiful tank in Siṃhaldvīpa. There he was informed that the king of that island, Pātaleśvara, had a daughter named Pāṭali, who, it was predicted should be married to a foreigner who would come there and whose name would be Putra. The young man understood what was meant. During the night, he secretly visited Pāṭali in her own apartment and told her who he was. The girl then agreed to go with him whenever he liked. Putra now wore his shoes, took Pāṭali on his back, and within a very short time arrived at a spot on the south bank of the Ganges, and west of the Puṇpuṇa. He was visited by the sage Nārada, who advised him to found a city and rule it by means of the rod. Putra then laid the foundation of a large city, and after him and his wife, called it Pāṭaliputra. Within a few years he conquered several provinces and became a great king. His mother had died of a broken heart. Putra's son Kusuma succeeded him, and during his time the city was called Kusumapura. Kusuma had a son Pāṭan, and a daughter Pātnā. After the name of the former, this city was for sometime called Patna. Pātnā did not marry, and was made a Devi by the gods, and is still the presiding goddess of the city, which is, after her, now called Pāṭnā. Putra, in his old days, left Pātnā with his wife and went to Kailas, where he made over to Mahādeva the three things which he had obtained from Sankaṭa and Bikaṭa. They lived hereafter in heaven. Such is the legendary account of the foundation of Pātnā.

Dr. Buchanan Hamilton records a local tradition that Sudarśana, who, "probably" was eighth in descent from Manu, bestowed the town on his daughter, Pāṭali, who cherished it like a son and hence called it Pāṭaliputra, and dedicated a temple to Paṭan Devi, the presiding goddess of the town. Mr. P. C. Mukharji, who refers to the above legend in his unpublished Report on the Excavations at Pāṭaliputra as well as to the antiquity of this town which, according to Diodorus, was founded by Hercules, observes, "The rational explanation of the legend appears to be that a citizen from Kusumpura built, after cutting a neighbouring forest, a garden house near a Pāṭali tree under which there was, as we generally see now, a rude representation of a sylvan deity, the archetype of Patan devi, where a fair was periodically held by the inhabitants. In the course of time, the suburb increased in importance, and a small village, Pāṭaligrāma, grew up associated with the legend of the Pāṭali tree; for the original builder of the garden-house was only remembered by the ignorant villagers as no other than the son or son-in-law of the spirit of the tree. Afterwards, when the rivers innundated and ruined Kusumputra, Pāṭaliputra became its natural successor." Mr. Mukharji's *A Report on the Excavations on the ancient sites of Pāṭaliputra in 1896-97*, was in proof only.

LECTURES III AND IV

The Edicts of Asoka

Mr. H. G. Wells, in an interview, an account of which appeared in an English Magazine, on the six *Greatest Men* in History spoke of Asoka among all the thousands of kings, emperors, and majesties, great and little, as shining almost alone, a star. "More living men cherish his memory to-day than have ever heard the name of Charlemagne"[1].

Asoka's position in History

It was, indeed, this *Raja-Chakravarti's* conversion to Buddhism which was the first and main cause of the position that Buddhists occupy in the history of humanity, and the widely-engraved Edicts[2] of the king all over his vast dominions, and his far-reaching efforts to extend Buddhism to the other civilised countries of the world, not only signify but attest the magnitude of his service to the cause of Buddhism.

His Edicts

Asoka, indeed, takes an honourable place in the gallery of the greatest kings known to history. It is not possible to discuss everything relating to Asoka, but he was, of course, pre-eminently the greatest king in ancient India. The political and religious grandeur of India commenced with him. The history of Indian Architecture must also date from Asoka, whose administrative ability has been highly and aptly praised. It was

---

1 *The Strand Magazine*, 1922. Dr. Sylvain Levi in his lecture on Ancient India, (*Journal of the Department of Letters*, Calcutta University, Vol. IX) observed: "Among the Kings of India there is one who eclipses even the most glorious."

2 "But for long centuries the characters in which his edicts are written were but lifeless letters; it needed a Prinsep to wring their secret from the stones grown mute and to bring to light that splendid period in which Hindu policy, encouraged and sustained by an active faith, claimed influence extending even to Cyrenaica, even to Epirus, on the confines of the Roman and the Carthaginian world." *Ibid.*

he who studded every part of his vast dominions, over which he wielded sovereignty as the paramount power, with pillars, *chaityas*, public halls, monasteries and splendid retreats and residences carved in the interior of the rocks. Within his dominions, there were many remarkable structures which excited the administration of foreigners, who came to India centuries after his death, and who characterised them as being built not by man, but by spirits[1]. Even after thousands of years, the stupendous ruins excite the admiration of one and all. I shall try to delineate here only one of the aspects relating to undoubtedly the greatest king of the land we live in, an aspect through which we can discern the "man of strong will, unwearied application, and high aims, who spared no labour in the pursuit of his ideals, possessed the mental grasp capable of forming the vast conception of missionary enterprise in three continents, and was at the same time able to control the intricate affairs of Church and State in an empire which the most powerful sovereign might envy"[2]. Indeed, his idea of engraving the Edicts, was, to say the least of it, original and bold, unparalleled in the realms of history, and has indeed satisfied the great king's earnest desire for perpetuating his measures, and—may we say—his name.

The aspects of the Edicts

With reference to these immortal Edicts the general idea is that they were meant only for the "long endurance" of the Good Law of Piety—or the *Dhamma*. This is evidently a narrow view, and it will surprise many of the audience to know that even the eleventh edition of that great work, the *Encyclopædia Britannica*, says, "The inscriptions which contain altogether about five thousand words, are entirely of religious import and their references to wordly affairs are incidental". Mr. Vincent Smith has also observed, "The inscriptions

1 *Travels of Fa-hien.*

2 V. A. Smith's *Asoka*, p. 106.

are all devoted to the exposition, exaltation and dissemination of the Law of Piety".[1] In fairness to this historian, however, it must be admitted that he has also incidentally referred to the importance of some Edicts from the point of view of political history. I will try to show, however, that not only from the point of view of religion, but from other points of view—political, social, and economic—the Edicts give us a very bright and clear picture of ancient India in the "golden age" of the Imperial Mauryas. It would, of course, not be possible for me to deal with the religious aspect of the Edicts, not that I ignore that, I cannot possibly do that,—indeed no one can—for Asoka stands beside St. Paul, Constantine and Omar, but, unfortunately, the time at my disposal allows me to touch the fringe of certain matters only. Perhaps on some other occasion, I may be permitted to do it. In this connection, it is a pleasure to mention the work of love done by a large number of European scholars in this field, as in other fields, to elucidate the mysteries of the Edicts. But the explanations and interpretations of

---

1 *Asoka*, p. 161. "His edicts, graven on rocks and pillars in all the provinces under his dominions, preach in simple and familiar language the loftiest lessons of goodness, gentleness, charity and mutual respect that humanity has ever heard. (Sylvain Levi in *Ancient India*.) For the editions of the Edicts :—

1877—Burgess.

1877—Cunningham : *Corpus*, Vol. 1.

1881—Senart : *Les Inscriptions de Piyadasi.* Vol. I (2nd edition, in 1888.)

1887—Bühler

1894—*Epigraphia Indica, Vol.* II.

1923—Hultzsch, new edition of *Corpus*, Vol. I.

See in this connection V. A. Smith's *Asoka*, 227—230.

For the comparative study of the Edicts, Senart, O. Franke, Fleet, Thomas, Smith, Hultzsch, Michelson, Bhandarkar and Lüders are to be mentioned. The recently published *Asokan Texts and Glossary* is a *vade mecum*.

many terms were not satisfactory till the discovery of the *Arthaśāstra*. So much has been written on this book, and we have also referred to it previously, that it would be superfluous to add anything on its importance from every point of ancient Indian History—political, social, and economic ; yet mention must always be made of the discovery of the great work of Chāṇakya by Dr. Shamaśāstry and his learned translation of the same. It would not also be altogether of out place to refer in this connection to the great German orientalist—I mean Dr. Jolly—whose edition of the *Arthaśāstra* is out, and the publication of which throws more light on the subject. Likewise, I would like to place on record an edition of the same *vademecum* by the late Dr. Ganapati Sāstri of Travancore, under the auspices of the enlightened ruler of that State[1]. The discovery of Kauṭilya's book has made still more possible a better understanding of the Edicts of Asoka, during the time of whose grandfather the great Viśṇugupta helped the beginning of what may be called the golden age of ancient India. But for this timely discovery, many a term in the Edicts would have been still shrouded in mystery. We have in these lectures tried to contribute our mite towards the explanation of some terms in the light of the *Arthaśāstra*.

The Edicts and the Arthaśāstra

I shall first draw your attention to some of these Edicts from the social point of view.

The social aspects of the Edicts

Sanctity of animal life along with duty to parents and superiors, was, of course, the cardinal doctrines of the Edicts. We find it repeated in many of them. Indeed, the first occupied the innermost place, in the heart of Asoka. Next to it was the duty to parents. In the second Minor Rock Edict, "Father and mother were to be hearkened to," an injunction which was repeated in the Third and Fourth Rock Edicts, as well

1 The sudden demise of Dr. G. Sāstri has caused a serious breach in the rank of orientalists.

as in the eleventh and thirteenth, for that was an "excellent thing". Similarly, duty to teachers was inculcated in Rock Edict II, as well as in Edict IX, while it was also enjoined that fitting courtesy was to be shown to relations whose unseemly behaviour was growing.

Slavery amongst the India

Due reverence is to be paid to superiors, but this does not indicate that slaves and servants are not to be meted out proper treatment. Rock Edict IX inculcates this doctrine. Indeed, if I may be permitted to enter into a digression, I may assert that the lot of slaves in ancient India—and this includes the Maurya times also—was, on the whole, pretty satisfactory. Megasthenes has observed that "the law ordains that none among Indians shall under any circumstances be a slave" [1]. The Grecian ambassador referred to the case of the Aryans only, but if the testimony of *Arthaśāstra* is to be accepted, we may say that an Ārya could be enslaved, though for four reasons only, *viz.*, capture, judicial punishment, voluntary self-degradation and debt. Slavery was, of course, in existence, but was not regarded as very humiliating, and the general condition of a slave was not a hard one. Chāṇakya lays down that "employing a slave to carry the dead or to sweep, or to give him the leavings of food, keeping a slave naked, or hurting or abusing him, or violating the chastity of a female slave shall cause the forfeiture of the value paid by him or her"[2]. But the son of an Ārya who enslaved himself would be still an Ārya.[3] Slaves could enjoy private property, and what was more, anything which a slave earned, without prejudice to his master's work, was the slave's property, and after his death was to go to his kinsmen, and the master

1 Megasthenes, McCrindle's edition.

2 *The Arthaśāstra*, III, 13.

3 *Ibid.*

was to get it only in the event of the slave having no kinsmen.[1]

There were again special regulations for boy-slaves, *i. e.*, boys who were less than eight years of age. They could not be mortgaged or sold in a foreign land, neither could such a slave be employed in any mean avocation. A slave could obtain liberty on payment of the price for which he was enslaved, and after that he could regain his Āryahood.[2]

Sanctity of animal life

Respect for living creatures, *i. e.*, sanctity of animal life, was naturally one of the cardinal doctrines of the great Buddhist king. We note in the Edicts the successive stages of his growing enthusiasm for his favourite doctrine : stopping of slaughter in the royal kitchen developed into prohibition, and gradually this puritanism gained more and more in strength, till after twenty-six years[3] he laid down an elaborate code practically prohibiting the slaughter of animals (even chaff was not to be burnt), a regulation in which there was no restriction of creed or custom.

The Testament of Asoka

Evidently Asoka had this sanctity of animal life in view, when he made healing arrangements for men as well as for beasts.[4] Medicinal herbs for men and for beasts, wheresoever lacking, were imported and planted ; for the same object also, wells were dug on the roads, and trees planted for the enjoyment of both men and beasts. Mr. Vincent Smith in this connection observes that "the sanctity attaching to the life of the most insignificant insect was not extended to the life of man."[5] But this view of the historian regarding the great King seems to be narrow. The second Rock

---

1 *Ibid.*

2 *The Arthaśāstra.*

3 Pillar Edict, V.

4 Girnār Rock Edict.

5 *Asoka*, p. 58.

Edict recounts the action of the monarch, conducive to the welfare *(Patibhoga)* of man as well as of beast, such as the digging of wells, the planting of banyan and mango trees, the erection of rest-houses and watering places, the provision of medicines for men as well as for lower animals. This conclusively shows that the King cared as much for animal life as for men, though it was animal life which he sought to save by promulgating the first Edict. The explanation is obvious. No importance had yet been attached to animal life. On the contrary, as we find clearly mentioned in the fourth Rock Edict, appreciatively characterised as *the Testament of Asoka*, "for a long period past, even for many hundreds of years, the sacrificial slaughter of living creatures, the killing of animate beings" had gone on increasing, and it was therefore only in the fitness of things, that the great Buddhist king who wanted to inculcate *ahiṃsā*, should devote more attention to animal life which had been neglected previously. But that does not, as we have just now observed, imply in any way that sanctity was not extended to the life of man—God's highest and noblest creation. As we find in the latter portion of the same Edict, "As for many hundred years before has not happened, now at this present, by reason of the inculcation of the *Dhamma* by his Sacred and Gracious Majesty the King, have increased abstention from the slaughter of living creatures, abstention from the killing of animate beings", or elsewhere as we find, it was "to attain release from my debt to animate beings", that he created the post of Censors. These did not show any disregard for human life. It was far from it.

No distinction, indeed, has been made between men and beasts, and, in fact, when we consider the nature of toleration inculcated by Asoka, we cannot accept the opinion of Mr. Smith, who compared the great

King with other Hindu rājās of later times, who did not hesitate to execute a man for killing a beast.[1] We need not believe in the monkish legend that Asoka abolished the death-penalty, for the extreme penalty of law, (taking it for granted that it did exist), is to be considered as an unavoidable necessity which could not, perhaps, be dispensed with.

Hospitals

Perhaps, we may refer in this connection to the expression "*Chikisā Katā Manuśa Paśu Chikisā Cha.*"[2] Bühler was the first who interpreted the word *Chikisā* as "hospitals". It is interesting to refer to the *Artha-śāstra*, where, in connection with buildings, Chāṇakya lays down that there should be hospitals within the fort. The sympathy of Asoka with his suffering fellow-creatures, both man and animal, finds adequate expression in the provisions made for the healing of man and beast, not only throughout his vast empire, but even in the kingdoms of his friends.[3]

And although we may not be prepared to go so far with Mr. V. A. Smith as to say that the animal hospitals which exist now-a-days may be regarded as either survivals or copies of the institutions founded by the Maurya Monarch, we may say that even in the time of the Chinese traveller, Fa-hien, there was in Pātaliputra an excellent free hospital, where "came all poor or helpless patients suffering from all kinds of infirmities ;"[4] these almost certainly had their origin in the days of the great Buddhist Monarch. Mr. Smith grows very eloquent over this and says, "It may be doubted if any equally efficient foundation was to be seen elsewhere in the world at that date ; and its

---

1 *Asoka*, p. 59.

2 Senart translated it into "remedies," Kern into "system of caring for the sick," Bhandarkar into "provisions or provident arrangements", and V. A. Smith into "curative" (healing) arrangements.

3 Rock Edict, II.

4 Fa-hien, *Travels*, XXVII.

existence, anticipating the deeds of modern christian charity, speaks well both for the character of the citizens who endowed it and for the genius of the great Asoka, whose teaching still bore some wholesome fruit many centuries after his decease".[1]

Toleration of Asoka

Toleration, in fact, was the characteristic and basis of the religious ideal of the great Emperor. Liberality towards ascetics and Brāhmaṇas was included in the ninth Rock Edict, a doctrine repeated in Edict XII, where it is inculcated that the "sects of other people all preserve reverence for one reason or other". "By acting thus, a man exalts his own sect and at the same time does service to the sects of other people. By acting contrariwise, a man hurts his own sect, and does disservice to the sects of other people. For, he who does reverence to his own sect, while disparaging the sects of others wholly from attachment to his own, with intent to enhance the splendour of his own sect, in reality, by such conduct inflicts the severest injury on his own sect".[2] While lavishing his treasure chiefly on Buddhistic shrines and monasteries, he did not hesitate to spend large sums in hewing out of hard-rocks spacious cave-dwellings for the Ājivikas, not even grudging the expense of polishing the interiors like so many mirrors and there can be no doubt that liberal benefactions were bestowed likewise on the Jains and Brāhmaṇas[3]. The *Arthaśāstra* has observed, "The king should follow the (conquered) people in their faith with which they celebrate their national, religious and congregational festivals or ornaments'.'[4] Asoka, indeed, has gone further than Chāṇakya. Kautilya provides no place for the heretics within

1 *The Early History of India*, p. 313.

2 Rock Edict, XII.

3 Kashmir tradition preserves the name of Brāhmaṇical temples built or restored by Asoka.

4 The *Arthaśāstra*, XIII, 5.

a fortress, except beyond the cremation grounds[1]. But in his Rock Edict, Asoka expresses his desire that persons professing all shades of belief may live anywhere they like ; for says the King, "all of them aim at self-control and purity of mind". That Asoka attached particular importance to toleration, is very much evidenced by the fact that Rock Edict XII which endeavours to impress upon every one the necessity for toleration towards all, has been constituted into a document by itself, being incised separately from the group. The connection between Rock Edict XI and Rock Edict XII lies in the fact that his subjects are asked to be tolerant towards the views of religious sects other than their own.

Existence of Torture

The word *Paliklesam*[2] occurs in the Dhauli Edict. Dhauli near Bhubanesvara, in Orissa, is a very important place in our province, having been identified with Tosali, one of the provincial capitals of Asoka[3]. This Edict inscribed in the fourteenth and fifteenth regnal years was addressed to the high officers administering the town. Mr. V. A. Smith referring to this word has translated it into "bodily torture" and comes to the conclusion that, "it is clear that Asoka maintained the ferocious criminal code of the *Arthaśāstra* and of his grandfather. He merely tried to remedy abuses in administration by admonition and supervision, but no man can tell how far he succeeded or failed". So far as the last part of the historian's conclusion goes, *i. e.*, "no man can tell how far he succeeded", every body has to concur, but I beg to differ from him about the other statement.

It is true that in the *Arthaśāstra* several chapters[4]

---

1 *Ibid*, II. 4.

2 Senart and Lüders have rendered into "serious trouble", while Bühler has "harsh treatment."

3 *J. B. & O. R. S.*, VIII. 5.

4 Book IV. 8.

do deal with the Mauryan Law on the question of judicial torture, but we also note there the following :

(*a*) Punishment is to be meted out only when the charge is quite established against the accused :

(*b*) A number of people such as ignoramuses, etc., and Brāhmaṇas could never be subjected to torture. Women also were generally excluded. Mr. Smith himself refers to the fact in the *Arthaśāstra* that when the Superintendent of Jails subjects any persons to unjust torture, he is to be fined ;[1] and causing death to anyone by torture was strictly prohibited[2].

Further, the Edict says that, "The administators of the town may strive all the time that the restraint or torture of the townsmen may not take place *without due cause*". This expression, *without due cause*, has been explained by Mr. Smith himself. If due regard had to be paid to the law, how could there be excessive torture ? There was the punishment for mutiliation, no doubt, but there was the alternative of fine. Only in one case we do find reference to a man being tortured to death, *viz*., when a man murdered another in a quarrel. Mr. Smith characterises all the eighteen kinds of torture referred to by Chāṇakya, as appalling. Of these eighteen, nine were strokes with a cane—a punishment which is even now resorted to. And if we compare the kinds of punishment in vogue even in the eighteenth century in other countries,[3] we cannot accept the conclusion of the author of *Asoka* who characterises the Mauryan Law as "horrible"[4].

---

1 *Ibid*, chap IX, p. 282.

2 *Ibid*, chap VIII, p. 278.

3 Cf. *e.g*. Lecky's *History of England* where an account has been given of the criminal law of England.

4 *Asoka*, p. 196.

And further, when we consider in this connection, that there were a number of humane regulations even to prevent cruel treatment to animals, we can have little justification for saying that Asoka maintained the ferocious criminal code of his ancestors. For the maintenance of good government punishment was and is necessary, but that he resorted to unnecessarily cruel measures is more than what we know of the great monarch[1].

Samāja and its explanation

In the first Rock Edict there is a term *Samāja*, which Dr. Thomas explained as "plainly a celebration of games or rather contests taking place in an arena, or amphitheatre, surrounded by platforms for spectators"[2]. And, if we enquire what there may have been in them to offend the humanity of Asoka, we have only to call to mind the contests of animals described by the Greeks and implied in Sanskrit literature. "The life of revelry indulged in by the warrior-caste, already indicated by the rules of drinking, dicing and contests between animals, and shown by the law, is perhaps caricatured by the great carousal in the *Harivamśa*, but is testified to not only by Megasthenes, but by the description in the Epic of all the paraphernalia of pastime at court. Majestic preparations! An amphitheatre for a joust at arms, moated and walled like a gated city; a cassino by the riverside for the amusement whenever any event offers an excuse; meat and wine at every festival; drunkenness, gambling and love, the enjoyments of peace"[3]. Dr. Thomas refers also to the *Dighanikāya*

1 Even in the days of Fa-hien, crimes were punished only by fines, varying in amount according to the gravity of the offence, and capital punishment seems to have been unknown. Only persons guilty of repeated rebellions suffered amputation of the right hand, but such a penalty was exceptional and judicial torture was not practised.

2 *Journal of the Royal Asiatic Society*, 1914, p. 394.

3 *Journal of the American Oriental Society*, XIII.

i. l. 14, where we have mention of fights between elephants, buffaloes, etc., and concludes, "we can easily, therefore, see why attendance at such gatherings is in the *Dighanikāya*[1] stigmatized as a sin".

Dr. Thomas, however, failed to notice one significant fact regarding this. The Edict says : "Here no animal may be slaughtered for sacrifice, nor shall any merry-makings be held. His Sacred and Gracious Majesty sees much offence, although certain merry-makings are excellent in the sight of His Sacred and Gracious Majesty the King." A *Samāja* was "a public feast where meat, as one of the principal articles of food, was served."[2]

But what was the other *Samāja* which a puritan king like Asoka thought excellent ? Evidently it must have been something where no animal life was sacrificed. In religious literature we find references to three descriptions of such a *Samāja*. The first reference is in the *Harivaṃśa*[3] where Kaṃśa invited his people to witness a wrestling match ; the second is in the *Mahābhārata*,[4] where Droṇāchāryya, the teacher of the Kuru-Pāṇḍavas, after finishing their education wanted to give a public exhibition and a *Samāja* was accordingly announced to the people ; the third description is also in the *Mahābhārata* in connection with the *Svayamvara* of Draupadi where a *Samāja* was held, with actors, dancers, etc[5]. Thus, so far as Brāhmaṇical literature is concerned, we meet with three kinds of *Samāja* all referring to the con-

1 III. 182.

2 *Indian Antiquary*, October, 1913. Cf. *Harivaṃśa* where Kṛṣṇa held in honour of the God Bilvodakeśvara, a *Samāja* which "abounded in a hundred varieties of meat and curry, was full of divers (kinds) of food and surcharged with condiments".

3 Verses 4528-4538 and 4642-4658.

4 Adi, Ch. XXXIV.

5 *Ibid*, CLXXXVII.

course of people assembled there. All the three were held by kings, and arrangements were made to make the people comfortable. "*Maṇchas* and *Paryaṇkas* were set up and different classes of people had different compartments assigned. Arrangements for drinking-water and stimulants were made. Actors, dancers and musical instruments were also brought in to feast their eyes and ears"[1].

In Buddhist literature, also, there were two kinds of *Samāja*, one, in which meat and other prohibited food were allowed, while in the other, there were only innocent amusements permitted ; *e. g.*, we find in *Vinaya*[2] certain *Bhikṣus* behaving like ordinary sensual laymen in a *Samāja*, while in another case,[3] we have an account of a *Samāja*, where the assembled *Bhikṣus* bathed and dined, there being no partaking of prohibited food or drink. Evidently the second kind of *Samāja* is referred to in the latter portion of the Edict which was appreciated by the king being considered as *Sādhumatā*.

Perhaps, here, you will allow me to make a little digression and refer to Dr. Thomas who, in his learned article in the *Journal of the Royal Asiatic Society*,[4] referred to above, observes : "It will be noted that the *Samāja* is frequently regarded as taking place on the top of a hill, concerning which it will be sufficient to refer to the paper of Hardy and the writers whom he quotes. As Hardy remarks," the sense of *giri* is eventually evaporated. Curiously enough, a theatrical meaning of the word may be traced in comparatively later times ; for commenting upon an anthology-verse from the *Mālati- Mādhava*, while, still ignorant of the history of

1 Prof. Bhandarkar in the *Indian Antiquary*, 1913.

2 II. 5, 2, 66.

3 IV. 37, 1.

4 1914, p. 394.

the matter, I have remarked, "Has this word also a theatrical signification ?"

The word, indeed, has a reference to theatrical performances. *Vātsāyana* in his *Kāmasūtra* says: "On the day of a fortnight or month, sanctioned by prevailing custom, those who are attached to the service of the temple of the Goddess of Learning must hold a *Samāja*. Actors coming from other places should give them a performance." And again in the *Jātaka*,[1] it appears that in those days there were companies of itinerant actors whose business was to move from place to place and show their performances which had also the same name[2].

Political aspects of the Edicts

Let us now direct our attention to a number of references to political history, indications of which are of great importance in studying the political atmosphere of those days. And it is a pleasure in this connection to note here the services rendered by Indian scholars, notably Prof. D. R. Bhandarkar, the worthy son of a worthy father, and Mr. K. P. Jayaswal, the well-known local Indologist. I shall discuss here some terms only, leaving aside those references which give us important information regarding the political history of the period, proving that Asoka was in close terms of friendship and relationship with the kings of Egypt, Syria, Macedonia and Epirus.

Let us take the Third Rock Edict which I consider to be important, if not the most important, from the political point of view, where there are a number of terms which call for special attention—*Yukta*, *Rājuka*, *Prādeśika*, *Anusaṃyāna*, *Pariśā* and *Gaṇanā*.

Dr. Thomas was the first to recognise the meaning of

---

1 No. 318.

2 Vide *Indian Antiquary*, 1918, the article of Mr. N. G. Majumdar where this question has been dealt with in a scholarly manner. Vide, *ante*. p. 25, where Puṣyamitra's Asvamedha has been referred to.

Yukta

Yukta[1] as a subordinate official. Both Chānakya's *Arthaśāstra*[2] and the *Mānava Dharmaśāstra*[3] confirm this explanation of the term. The next is *Rājuka,* who, as we see in the Fourth Pillar Edict, had power over many hundred thousands of people. Bühler's notion of its relation to *rajju*, a measuring rope, was evidently mistaken[4]. Mr. Vincent Smith has translated the term as "Governor." He says that, "considering the extent of these officers' powers over hundreds of thousands of subjects, and the unfettered discretion allowed to them, the rendering "Governors" is preferable to "Commissioners"[5].

Rājuka

This may or may not be right, but evidently he is not correct in saying that the designation *Rājuka* does not occur in the *Arthasāstra.* It does; if we refer to page 293 of the English Edition[6], we find the term. "Whatever of their (traders') merchandise is stolen or lost in the intervening places between any two villages shall the Superintendent of pasture-lands make good. If there are no pasture-lands (in such places), the officer called *Chorarajjuka* shall make good the loss. If the loss of merchandise occurs in such parts of a country as are not provided even with such security (a *Chorarajjuka*), the people in the boundaries of the place shall contribute to make up the loss"[7]. It is therefore likely that the post of *Rājuka* had long existed and that Asoka's innovation consisted in granting them extensive

1 *J. R. A. S.*, 1909 and 1914, p. 387. According to Dr. Bhandarkar, *Asoka*, p. 53, they were district officers who managed the king's property, received and kept accounts of the revenue and had powers to spend where expense was likely to lead to increase of revenue.

2 P. 70.

3 VIII. 34.

4 Cf. *Journal of the Royal Asiatic Society*, 1895, p. 661.

5 *Asoka*, p. 203.

6 Original, p. 232.

7 The term *Choravajju* (ropes to bind thieves) occurs in the *Arthaśāstra*, p. 66 (English Edition).

power without the necessity of obtaining sanction for particular acts by references to the Crown.[1] As the King observes "I have made rewards and punishments by the *Rājukās*, dependent on themselves" and this clearly explains their high position.

Prādeśika

The next term is *Prādeśika* which has been explained by Dr. Thomas as "an officer attached to the several grades of councillors and of local Governors, and charged with executive duties of revenue-collection and police, a combination so constant in India". Mr. Vincent Smith[2] accepts the explanation of Dr. Thomas and considers the officer "to have been more or less equivalent to the District Officer or Magistrate and Collector of modern India."

I venture to differ from both these high authorities. My first submission is that the word *Prādeśika* is derived from *Pradeśa* which evidently implies a division or a larger area—a fact which Dr. Thomas himself admits,[3] and secondly, if we refer to page 279[4] of the English translation of the *Arthaśāstra*, we find that Commissioners, *i. e.*, the *Pradeṣṭṛs*-officers whom Dr. Thomas has identified with these *Prādeśikas*—were to hold in check the Superintendents and their subordinates. They were, of course, under the Collector-General, as is evident from the above, but, that they wielded enormous powers is also clear[5], for we find that three commissioners[6] or three ministers shall deal with measures to suppress disturbance to peace. We find these officers doing also the duties of a judge.[7] Thus it appears that

1 Cf. *Z. D. M. G.*, XLVII, 466 ff. Also, Fick's *Social Organization* (English translation, Calcutta University, pp 148-149).

2 *Asoka*, p. 162.

3 *J R. A. S.*, 1914, p. 384.

4 Cf. Pages 142 & 220 of the original.

5 P. 200 of the original, p. 253 of the translation.

6 *Pradeṣṭṛs*.

7 Pp. 282 and 285 of the translation ; pp. 220 and 226 of the original

their position was equal to that of a minister and we are led to say that, considering the derivation of the word as well as the scope of their powers, they could not have been merely "district" officers charged with executive duties of revenue collection and police"[1], but their position was evidently more important and they were very likely equal in position to the modern Commissioners.

Anusamyāna

The Girnār and the Kaliṅga Edicts contain the term *Anusaṃyāna*. This is a difficult term and the difficulty has been intensified by the fact that up to this time the word has been found used but rarely[2]. At one time, the word was translated as "assembly" and on another occasion as "circuit". A new explanation has been suggested by Mr. K. P. Jayaswal in the *Journal of the Bihar and Orissa Research Society*[3]. He asks, "Would the whole body of the High Ministers, who, as at Taxila and at Ujjain, were charged with the Government of the Presidency or Viceroyalty, "go out" or "be turned out" together "for the propose of going on an official tour?" And he goes on to observe that "the result would be that the Capital would be without a single minister during the alleged 'tour'." This interpretation was accepted by the late Dr. V. A. Smith who observes[4], "He is probably correct in referring to the *S'ukranīti* and interpreting the term as signifying a regular system of transfer from one station or district to another, designed to prevent the abuses apt to arise

1 *Asoka*, p. 164.

2 *Vide* The Pali Text Society's *Pali English Dictionary*, p. 43.

3 IV. 36 ff. I have been severely taxed for having ventured to differ from this learned interpretation, but I am glad to find that the *Asoka Text and Glossary* thus writes : "Jayaswal in succession or transfer (60 r. 4. 37 quotes *S'ukranīti* II. 107—113) but this is contrary to usual meaning of verbs with *Anu* and *Sam* and to the use with the *abl.* Moreover the sense of "tour" for inspection purposes fits all passages and the general custom."

4 *Asoka*, p. 164.

when officials remain too long in a particular locality." There are certain aspects of the question which have to be discussed before the proposed interpretation can be accepted as final.

The first thing we have to note is how far the *S'ukranīti* is to be considered as an authority. It is a very late work which I would hesitate very much to depend on. Secondly, there is no mention of cabinet-ministers in the passage of the *S'ukranīti* referred to by Mr. Jayaswal[1] who writes, "The *S'ukranīti* provides for the transfer of cabinet-ministers with their two Under-Secretaries every three, five, seven or ten years". The passage as translated by Prof. B. K. Sarkar[2] is as follows :—"He should always appoint three men for each department, the wisest of them all at the head and two others as overseers, for three, five, seven or ten years, and having noticed each officer's qualification for the work entrusted, he should make the necessary changes. The king should never give office for ever to anybody and everybody. He should appoint men to offices after examining the fitness of the persons for them, for who does not get intoxicated by drinking of the vanity of office ?"[3] As this translation does not appear to be very literal, I venture to translate it as follows : "There should be one chief officer, under whom there will be two overseers of that department. The transfer is to be effected after 3, 5, 7 or 10 years. His

1 *J. B. & O. R. S*, Vol. IV, p. 37.

2 *Sacred Books of the Hindus Series.*

3 Prof. B. K. Sarkar adds the following note.—"Here are rules for the management of each *Adhikāra* or jurisdiction; *i.e.*, department. *Darśaka*—inspectors, overseers. *Hāyana*—years. The term of office or tenure of appointment is for 3, 5, 7 or 10 years according to *Kāryyakauśalya, i.e.*, qualification. S'ukrāchāryya warns the king against bestowal of permanent offices. Appointments to posts should be according to time, during good behaviours. If the pride of position bewilders the officer and he proves unworthy of the responsibility, he should be dismissed. Work is the sole test and recommendation for office."

(*i. e.* the officer's) work and cleverness in doing it have to be considered in transferring him. Seeing that he is fit for that post, he is to be appointed to that post, for every man gets intoxicated by enjoying a post for a long time. For that purpose he is to be appointed to some other post, provided that he is fit for it"[1]. Mr. Jayaswal may be right in assuming that "a defined period of office was regarded as a salutary provision as reminding the ministers of their limited sojourn and making them mindful of their responsibility,"[2] but may I submit my reasons for not taking his view about the other point ?

First, I beg to refer to the *S'ukranīti* itself where the king is advised to appoint his chief advisers to each post by *rotation*[3]. There does not seem to be any question of *going out*. And the reason is explained in the next *sloka* which says that "the king should not make his officers more powerful than himself."

There is another reason, and a very strong one, and this we can trace in the Edicts themselves. In the very Edict where the term occurs, we are told that the officers were not only to proceed for their lay business but also for the special purpose of inculcating the Law of Piety. The Provincials' Edict also lays down that "in accordance with the Law of Piety, I shall send forth *in rotation*,[4] every five years, such persons as are of mild and temperate disposition, and regardful of the sanctity of life, who knowing this my purpose will comply with my instructions". And it continues : "when the High Officers aforesaid......proceed on transfer in rotation, then without neglecting their own (ordinary) business, they will attend to this matter also and thus will carry out the King's

1 I am indebted to my colleague, Prof. S. N. Majumdar Sāstri, for helping me to translate it.

2 *J. B. & O. R. S.*, IV. 39.

3 II, 107 and 108. *Paribardha* is the term used.

4 These very terms have been used in the *S'ukranīti*.

instructions". And when we consider in this connection that the great King Asoka himself had tours of piety, when he visited ascetics and Brāhmaṇas,[1] with gifts made to them, rewarded elders with largesses of gold, visited the people of the country for instructing them in the Law of Piety and discussion of that Law, we can safely say that his subordinates also, from the *Rājukās* downwards, had to perform these tours of piety. Taxila and Ujjain were too far off from the capital and hence the tours of piety to these two places were to be undertaken after 3 years, *i. e.*, shorter periods[2] had to be observed in view of the distance from the capital.

Tours of Piety

The term *Gaṇanāyam* is also important. It was the Department of Accounts referred to in the *Arthaśāstra*[3]. The business of keeping accounts in the office of the Accountants gives us full details about this department, one of its duties being to prevent the diminishing of revenue—"excellent is small expense with small accumulation". As Kauṭilya says, "By how much the Superintendent of a department augments the net total of its revenue either by increasing any one of the items of its receipts or by decreasing any one of the items of expenditure, he shall be rewarded with eight times that amount. But when it is reversed (*i. e.*, when the net total is decreased) the award shall also be reversed (*i. e.*, he shall be made to pay eight times the decrease'[4], the object in every case being economy. Indeed, a wise Collector-General was to conduct the work of revenue-collection, by increasing the income and decreasing the

Gaṇanāyam

1 Rock Edict, VIII.

2 Mr. V. A. Smith observes, "We cannot explain with certainty why it was thought necessary to transfer the officials in the outlying provinces every three years." *Asoka*, p. 197. I venture to submit the above explanation.

3 *The Arthaśāstra*, II. 7.

4 *The Arthaśāstra*, I. XII.

expenditure"[1]. Obedience to father and mother, liberality to friends, acquaintances, relatives, Brāhmaṇas and ascetics, abstention from the slaughter of living creatures are all of the same value as small expenditure. These were all *Sādhu* or sacred and excellent duties.

Mr. Jayaswal has in this connection observed that the *Gaṇanā, i. e.*, the Department of State Accounts, was required to take notes of the order of the five-yearly transfers, implying that no allowance to the ministers after the fifth years was to be sanctioned by the Department, as that would be unlawful expenditure. In view of what we have already quoted from the *Arthaśāstra* and what we find in its eighth chapter regarding the deductions of what is embezzled by government servants out of State revenue and that "all undertakings depend upon finance" which all point categorically to the very great importance of saving money, there may be, however, some connection between the above two. But who were supreme—the *Gaṇanā* or the ministers? Were the ministers, whom Mr. Jayaswal has endowed with all executive powers, and who according to him were even more powerful than the King himself, at the mercy of the Department of Accounts? If the ministers were so powerful, how could they be at the mercy of that Department?

Parisā

The term *Parisā* in this Edict is also one which requires further examination. Senart took it as *Saṃgha* and Bühler as the "committee of the caste". The latest interpretation is *Mantri parisat—parisat of the Mahāmātras*. This term has been used in the *Arthaśāstra*[2]. Kauṭilya observes, "All kinds of administrative measures were to be preceeded by deliberations

---

1 *Ibid*, II. 6

2 I. XV. Lassen, "the assembly of the doctors," Senart, "the clergy" and Bühler, "the teachers and ascetics of all schools" and "committee of the caste or sect."

in a well-formed Council"[1]. And again, "in works of emergency, the King shall call both his ministers and the assembly of ministers"[2]. Mr. Jayaswal referring to these considers that the Council of Ministers was very powerful, so much so, that the Emperor was deprived of "authority" by the ministers[3].

But how far was this Council of Ministers effective? Is it not that too much prominence has been given to the existence of the ***Mantriparisat*** with which has been compared the modern Executive Councils? Regarding this important question, Kautilya has observed that the King is not to despise anybody's opinion[4], "for a wise man shall make use of even a child's utterance", and that "the King should despise none but hear the opinion of all."[5] He has also advised the formation of a well-formed Council in which all kinds of administrative measures were to be preceeded by deliberations[6]. We

Mantriparisat

1 *The Arthaśāstra, I. XV.*

2 *Ibid.*

3 *J. B. & O. R. S.*, IV. 43. See, also, Radhagovinda Basak's *Ministers in Ancient India, Indian Historical Quarterly, Vol. 1.*

4 *The Arthaśāstra*, I. XV.

5 *Ibid.*

6 *Ibid.* The authority which Chāṇakya exercised over Chandragupta, as we find in the *Mudrārākṣasa*, furnishes subsidiary evidence about this. Kauṭilya argues that " a single minister proceeds wilfully and without restraint", and, as such, he might have advocated the Council. In the Drama, however, we observe him always acting most wilfully and absolutely without any restraint. We see him exclaim :—

"All public acts possess
A threefold source,
And from the King, the minister,
Or both, can jointly emanate.
What I have done,
Is done by virtue of the State I hold :
And to enquire of me why I did it,
Is but to call my judgment or authority
In question and designedly affront me."

But even in trivial matters we find him interfering. The offended King observes :—

"If thus my highest mood is to be canvassed,

can, however, hardly accept what he says, *viz.* "in works of emergency the king shall call both his ministers and the assembly of ministers, or he shall do whatever course of action leading to success they point out". Here also suggestion or pointing out is to be done by the ministers, while the final action is to be taken by the King.

Further, what he lays down in Book V, Chapter 6, also supports the idea that he was really averse to a council. "The Minister is to install the heir-apparent, he is to conduct the administration, he is to invest himself with the powers of sovereignty". The Minister was all powerful no doubt, but *not* the Council of Ministers. And further : "it is verily the King who attends to the business of appointing ministers, priests and other servants, including the Superintendents of all departments" [1] This clearly shows who it was that was to wield the *real* power.

And lastly when he says, "the King shall employ ministers and *hear* their opinion"[2], we have clearly and categorically his verdict.

Hindu S'āstras including the *Rāmāyaṇa*[3], also fully corroborate us. In the *Mahābhārata*[4] as well, we find that there was one minister, Bhīsma, alone guarding the kingdom during the minority of the King. The Epic very clearly observes, "Even one single minister who is intelligent, heroic, self-controlled and discriminating, confers the greatest good on a king or king's son."

And thwarted by Your Excellency, my Kingdom
Is but a prison to me".
And Chāṇakya defiantly replies :
"It is ever thus
When monarchs reign with delegated sway".
Chāṇakya's machinations in getting hold of tbe minister Rākṣasa who is called "the hereditory councillor" (*S'ukraniti* also refers to such councillors) support our contention that there was no such Council.

1 *The Arthaśāstra*, VIII. I.

2 *Ibid*, I. 7.

3 Ayodhyā, C.

4 Sabhā, V.

And again, "Let the king appoint seven or eight ministers whose ancestors have been royal servants[1], who are versed in the sciences, heroes skilled in the use of weapons and descended from noble families and who have been tried. Let him consider with them the ordinary business (referring to) peace and war, (the four subjects called) *Sthāna*, the revenue, the (manner) of protecting (himself and his kingdom) and the sanctification of his gain (by pious gifts). *But with the most distinguished among them, a learned Brāhmaṇa, let the king deliberate on most important affairs which relate to the six measures of royal policy.* Let him, full of confidence, always entrust to that (official) all business. Having taken his *final resolution* with him, *let him begin to act.*" There is also here no mention of the executive powers of the ministers.

Executive powers of the Mantri-parisat

In later times, though we occasionally hear of a body of councillors, we are led to think that this body was more for show than for the exercise of any real power. For example, in the *Harṣacharita*, we do find mention of a council, but it met *once in five years* and that would conclusively prove our contention that the *Mantripariśat* had no executive powers.[2]

Too much importance has been attached to a passage in the *Divyāvadāna*[3], and Mr. V. A. Smith also seems to have accepted this view[4]. In fact, the theory regarding the executive power wielded by the *Parisat* is *practically* based on this passage, which literally translated, runs thus:—"The king to-day has been deprived of authority by his servants." As against this, let us turn to page 430

1 Cf. in this connection what we have quoted on p. 94, from *Mudrārākṣasa* about "*hereditory councillors*". This we consider to be significant.

2 In *Śukranīti* we do not find executive powers being wielded by ministers; only advisory powers are referred to. (II. 3 & 4.)

3 P 432, Cowell's edition.

4 *Asoka*, p. 164.

of the same book, the *Divyāvadāna.* There we find that the king resolved to give a thousand millions of gold pieces to the Master's service, and when far advanced in years, had actually given nine hundred and sixty millions. In the hope that the vow would be completed before he would die, Asoka daily sent great treasures of silver and gold to the *Kukkuṭārāma* monastery at the capital.[1]

At the time, Sampadi, the son of Kuṇāla, was the heir-apparent. To him the ministers said that the King was ruining himself by his extravagance, and would, if permitted to continue it, be unable to resist the attacks of other monarchs or to protect the kingdom. The prince, therefore, forbade, the treasurer to comply with the King's demands.[2] Two things may be noted here about the word *(Abhihitam)* used: This has been translated into "*pointed out*" by V. A. Smith, though "*said*" is the proper word. Whatever it may be, it does not indicate the wielding of executive powers by the ministers. Secondly, the executive power was, in fact, actually wielded by the heir-apparent who prohibited the treasurer and who had his own interests to look after.

Mr. Jayaswal then observes: 'The Edict which is practically an administrative one, exhibits the *Emperor's dissatisfaction at the restiveness o his ministers with regard to his certain commands.*" If so, what does it indicate? He was in the hands of the Ministers[3]. The action of the Ministers was evidently unauthorised; the term "*usurp*" clearly shows it. If we are to attach any importance to Hieun Tsiang, it was of no use to the King to show this fruitless restiveness, while if we take

1 Hieun Tsiang tells us that Asoka thrice gave away and purchased back *Jambudvīpa.* Beal, II, 91.

2 *Asoka,* p. 268.

3 Cf. Hieun Tsiang, Beal II. 96. "Whilst the fever has his person, his avaricious ministers have usurped his power and amassed wealth not their own".

the contrary case of his being unfettered by the council, could show restiveness in that his commands were not being carried out.

The learned Indolgist goes on : "That the ministers had such wide powers as to be in a position to offer opposition in certain matters, can be gathered by the data of the Greek writers". In a foot-note, he refers to two facts. First, that "this explanation supports the tradition of the *Divyāvadāna* (apart from other considerations, should so much importance be given to the *Divyāvadāna* which after all, embodies legends only ?) that Radhāgupta opposed the gifts of the King to the Buddhist Brotherhood." We have previously discussed this fact and we need not revert to it. In the second footnote, he gives a quotation from Arrian[1]. "Hence (the Councillors of State who *advise* the King) enjoy the prerogative of choosing the governor, chiefs of provinces, deputy governors, superintendents of the treasury, generals of the army, admirals of the navy, controllers and commissioners who superintend agriculture"[2]. The word actually used by Arrian is "*deliberate*" *i, e.*, they had merely advisory and no executive powers, and so Mr. Jayaswal's theory does not appeal to us. It is a far cry.[3]

1 Arrian, *Indika*, XII.

2 *The Arthaśāstra*, VIII. I, lays down clearly that it was verily the king who attended to the business of appointing ministers, priests and other servants, including the superintendents of several departments.

3 In Didot's edition of Arrian *Anabasis et Indica*, 1846, p. 213, the word in question means 'to deliberate', 'to hold deliberation on. The translation published in the *Indian Antiquary*, Vol. VI, p. 124, is, "The seventh caste consists of the Councillors and Assessors who deliberate on public affairs". That the king was the final arbiter is also accepted by Dr. Bhandarkar, *Asoka*, p. 61, where he says, "when he issues an oral order, or when any pressing matter devolves upon a *Mahāmātra*, the Parishad has to meet and discuss it. If they come to an unanimous decision, no question can arise as to its being carried out. But if there is a divergence of opinion or even unanimous opposition and the matter shelved for the time being, it is for the king to see what this difference or opposition is and find out which of their counsels

Pativedaka

The *Arthaśāstra* has laid special stress on spies and spy-system. Indeed, the institution of spies formed a special item in Chāṇakya's Code of Law. In the Sixth Rock Edict (Girnār), occurs the word *Paṭivedaka* which has been rendered into *ushers* by Mr. Jayaswal. According to Mr. V. A. Smith the reading is not quite satisfactory."[1] But Mr. Smith himself did not suggest any interpretation. Megasthenes, quoted by Strabo, speaks of the overseer, to whom was assigned the duty of watching all that went on and of making reports secretly to the King. The ablest and most trustworthy men were appointed to fill these offices.[2] I have my doubts regarding this latest interpretation. I am not aware of any such term having been used by Chāṇakya, but I am led to think that the term refers to spies, many of whom had free access to the King. We are told by the *Arthaśāstra*[3] that those spies "who are of good family, loyal, reliable, well-trained in the art of putting on disguises appropriate to countries and trades, and are possessed of knowledge of many languages and arts, shall be sent by the king to espy in his own country the movements of his ministers, priests, commanders of the army, the heir-apparent, the door-keepers, the officer-in-charge of the harem, the magistrate, collector-general, the chamberlain, the commissioner, the city-constable, the officer-in-charge of the city, the superintendent of transactions, the superintendent of manufactories, the assembly of councillors, heads of departments, the commissary-general and officer-in-charge

---

is most likely to be efficacious...... The Parishad was thus like a modern secretariat which was an intermediate administrative body between the king and the Mahāmātras....... If any division arose between them or even unanimous decision was reached, but contrary to that of the king or the Mahāmātras, the whole case was to be forwarded to the king as he was the final arbiter."

1 V. A. Smith, *Asoka*, p. 174.

2 V. A. Smith in the second edition of his *Asoka* had accepted the word *Paṭivedaka* in the sense of spies.

3 Book 1, Chap. XII.

of fortifications, boundaries and wild tracts. We are further informed that, "spies such as are employed to hold the royal umbrella, vase, fan and shoes, or to attend at the throne, chariot, and conveyance, shall espy the public character of these officers." Evidently, therefore, these spies would be the most proper persons to be always in touch with the king, to keep him informed, without the least delay, in all things which would be worth communicating to the king. If any had ready access to the king, if any had the chance of approaching easily both the king and the people, they would be very likely these *paṭivedakas*.

My proposed interpretation is supported by the fact that the word *Parisat*, which has been rendered into *Mantriparisat*, occurs in the above list given by Chāṇakya[1] and figures in this Edict also as *Parisā*. Special injunctions are laid down in the Sixth Rock Edict : "A long period has elapsed during which in the past, business was not carried on or information brought in at all times. So by me the arrangement has been made that at all times, when I am eating or in the ladies' appartments, or in my private room or in the mews, or in my conveyance, or in the pleasure-grounds, everywhere *the persons appointed to give information should keep me informed about the people*"[2]. The persons appointed to give information (and this is the meaning we get from the derivation of the word *Paṭivedaka*) could be very likely these spies. Ordinary ushers (whatever may be the duties of the gentlemen-ushers of the English court) could not Spies

1 *Vide, The Modern Review*, Calcutta, January, 1915.

2 Cf. The *Arthaśāstra* : 1. XII. "Spies shall also know the rumours prevalent in the State." Cf.also what Durmūkha did in the case of Sītā in *Uttara Rāma Charita*.

3 See *I. A.*, 1908, p. 53 and *Ibid*, 1920,53ff.

4 Dr. Shamasastri thinks that Mr. Jayaswal's interpretation is a forced one.

5 See *Indian Antiquary*, 1908, p. 53 and 1920, pp. 53ff.

have done so in the time of the Mauryas when the king as we find in the Greek accounts, could not sleep twice in one room, was so much afraid of his life, and when the spy system being so much in existence could be, had to be and was, so easily accessible.

The Edict goes on, "And in all places I attend to the affairs of the people. And, if, perchance, by word of mouth I personally command a donation or injunction; or again, when a matter of urgency has been committed to the high officers, and in that matter a division or adjournment takes place in the council, then without, delay, information must be given to me in all places, at all times."[1] I may be permitted to draw your attention to two aspects. First, if the latest argument about the supposed powers of the *Mantriparisat* is correct, then it was only natural that spies were to watch the movements and report these to the King. They are also distinctly asked to watch the movements of the Assembly of Councillors[2]. Secondly, even if the powers were executive, it was these *Paṭivedakas* who were required to inform the King that a difference in opinion had arisen. And we can take it, that in both cases the information was bound to please the King. It was only possible for the spies to carry such information to the King immediately, wherever he was.

Coming to the Fifth Rock Edict, we find the word *Mahāmātra* which is also referred to in Rock Edict XII

Mahāmātra

and Pillar Edict VII. Asoka observes: "Now in all the long time past, officers known as Censors (*Dhamma-mahāmātras*) of the Law of Piety never had existed, whereas such Censors were created by me." This implies that before Asoka's time, there were officers whose duty was confined to the ordinary business of administration, but Asoka introduced an innovation by

1 Rock Edict, VI.

2 Cf. *The Arthaśāstra*, 1-1-3, "Having set up spies over his *Mahāmātras*."

creating officers whose duty was to look to the Law of Piety, and with a similar object he created women-censors whose functions were directed towards ladies, the same functions as those which were exercised by Censors of the other sex towards men. We are told in Edict V that they were employed in the capital and in all provincial towns, in the female establishments of the King's brothers and sisters, as well as of other relatives. It is however, possible that the appointment of Censors to look after the morals of the women was a later development, for, at the time of the Fifth Rock Edict, the duty of superintending the female establishments of the royal family was left in the hands of the officials responsible for the general enforcement of the Law of Piety.

There was a well-conducted department under these Censors of the Law of Piety, who possessed the power of modifying the sentences of convicts, while their other duties included jurisdiction in cases of injury inflicted on animals contrary to the regulations, exhibitions of gross filial disrespect, and other breaches of the moral rules prescribed by authority. They were also instructed to redress cases of wrongful confinement or corporal punishment, and were empowered to grant remission of sentence when the offender was entitled to consideration by reason of advanced years, sudden calamity or having the burden of a large family. Very likely, they also shared with the Censors of women the delicate duty of supervising the morals of females, the households of the royal family both at the capital and in the provincial towns, being subject to their inspection[1].

By a study of the Edicts, we can, for all practical purposes, place before you the list of officers in the establishment of Asoka. A reference is also given showing who among the officers are mentioned by the *Arthaśāstra.*

---

1 *Asoka*, p. 99.

Viceroys

First comes, of course, the Viceroys who stood at the head of all officers. They were members of the royal family, with headquarters at Taxila, Tosali and Ujjain. There was also a fourth Viceroy, very likely at Suvannagiri, who ruled the southern provinces beyond the Nerbuddā.

Mahāmātras

The *Mahāmātras* came next, whose functions purely were lay, but a new class of them, who did both sorts of work, was organised by Asoka[1]. Next to them came the *Rājukās*, who, as we find in the Fourth Pillar Edict, were set over many hundred thousands[2] of people and were granted independence in the award of honours and penalties in order that they might confidently and fearlessly perform their duties, look after the welfare and happiness of the people in the country, confer favours upon them, and have independence in the awards of honours and penalties[3].

It seems to me that these were the officers who administered the central regions of the empire, while the Wardens of the Marches were the *Mahāmātra Prādeśikas*[4], whom Dr. Vincent Smith would classify as District officers, but who, evidently, as we have already ventured to show, seem to have been more like the Commissioners. We have the *Mahāmātras* of the Edicts[5], corresponding to the *Āmatyas* of the *Arthaśāstra*, while the term *Mahāmātra* occurs also in Kauṭilya[6].

---

1 Rock Edict, V. Pillar Edict, VII.

2 The high officers administering the town of Tosali were "set over many thousands of living beings." (Dhauli Edict.)

3 My idea is that as in the case of Censors, there were two sorts, one for ordinary business and the other for the Law of Piety, so there were also two sorts of *Rājukās*, one, for transacting ordinary business and the other for inculcating the *Dhamma*, as is clear from Pillar Edict VII. "In such and such a manner expound my teaching to the body of subordinate officials of the Law".

4 Rock Edict, III.

5 Rock Edict, V.

6 *The Arthaśāstra*, II. V.

In my second lecture I attempted to place before you the designations of officers mentioned by Megasthenes and compared their position, etc., as given by Chāṇakya. I shall try here to give designations of the officers mentioned in the Edicts of Asoka and see whether they have been mentioned by the author of the *Arthaśāstra*.

Gopas

In the Third Rock Edict, we have the *Yuktas*, the subordinate officials who very probably were the Gopas[1] who were to keep the accounts of ten households, with the duty of knowing the castes, *gotras*, the names and occupations of both men and women in those households as well as their income and expenditure. These subordinate officials might have also included the *Sthānikas* who were to attend to the accounts of the four quarters of the capitals. At any rate, the lowest class was the *Upayuktas* over which there were the *Yuktas*,[2] and considering their duties, the *Yuktas* of the Edicts[3] were the same as the *Yuktas* of the *Arthaśāstra*. These were all trained local officials[4].

Sthānika

Then came the *Nagalabichohalaka*[5] of the Edicts corresponding to the *Nāgaraka* or the town clerk of the *Arthaśāstra*. The *Mūkhas* of the Edicts[6] are, of course, the various Superintendents mentioned in Chapter XIII and XIV of the second Book and of which we have a fairly exhaustive list. We have mentioned them in our second lecture.

The Wardens of the Marches

The Wardens of the Marches as mentioned in the Edicts—*Anta Mahāmātras* appear in the *Arthaśāstra*

1 *Ibid*, II. XXXVI. There was another class of officers, named Puruṣa, denoting officials of various descriptions. In Pillar Edict 1, Asoka divides these Puruṣas into three classes as they are of the high, middle and low ranks.

2 *Ibid*, II. 5.

3 Rock Edict, VI.

4 The Borderers' Edict.

5 Rock Edict, VI. To some, he appears to have been a judge for district towns only. Bhandarkar, *Asoka*, p. 56.

6 Pillar Edict, VII.

as *Antapāla*[1] (though Mr. Vincent Smith observes that "they have not been heard of before by name")[2], with duties to guard the entrances into the kingdom. In the Edicts, their business was the observance of the Law of Piety. But may we not surmise that like some other officials their duties were both lay and ecclesiastical? The very fact of their being placed at the extremities of the Empire show that their principal duty was the protection of the Empire from attacks, while they might also have been employed to inculcate the Law of Piety upon people of the neighbouring states.

The sixth Rock Edict is also important from the political point of view. Here we find a close resemblance between what Asoka lays down and what Chāṇakya, the *Guru* of the Mauryas, lays down in his *Arthaśāstra.* Asoka was not at all content with what his officers did. Information was to be sent to him even if he was eating, or when he was in the ladies' apartments or wherever else he might be. The *Arthaśāstra* clearly lays down the duties of the king thus: "When in court, he shall never cause his petitioners to wait at the door, for, when a king makes himself in accessible to his people and entrusts his work to his immediate officers, he is sure to engender confusion in business and to cause thereby public disaffection, and himself a prey to his enemies. He shall, therefore, personally attend to the business of gods, of heretics, of Brāhmaṇas learned in the Vedas, of cattle,

Duties of kings

1 II—1. According to Bhandarkar, *Asoka*, p. 58, "These officials were not in charge of the frontier provinces of Asoka's empire, but rather those sent to the neighbouring stations and charged with the carrying out of Asoka's programme of Dhamma." He supports this by referring to the fact that in Pillar Edict I, Asoka distinguishes *Anta Mahāmātras* from Puruṣas or officers of his dominions and he goes on, "It further agrees with the fact that in Asoka inscriptions wherever the word *anta* occurs, it has the sense of either "a bordering King," or, "people of a bordering kingdom." Bühler takes them, as overseers of the frontier provinces," while Hultszch has "*māhāmtras* of the borders."

2 *Asoka*, p. 199.

3 For a list of the officers mentioned by Chāṇakya, see *Indian Historical Quarterly*, Vol. I p. 530.

of sacred places, of minors, of the aged. the afflicted, the helpless, and of women. All this in order (of enumeration) or according to the urgency or pressure of those works. All urgent calls he shall hear at once, and never put off, for when postponed, they will prove too hard or impossible to accomplish. Of a king, the religious vow is his readiness to action; satisfactory discharge of duties is his performance of sacrifice; equal attention to all in the offer of fees and ablution towards consecration. In the happiness of his subjects lies his happiness; in their welfare his welfare; whatever pleases himself he shall not consider as good, but whatever pleases his subjects he shall consider as good! Hence the king shall ever be active in the discharge of his duties." If we thus compare the two—the Edicts and the *Arthaśāstra*—it would appear that the great Buddhist Emperor copied the dictates of the great Brāhmaṇa minister. Indeed, Asoka was only following the *Nītiśāstras* or the principles of Government, *Nīti*, referred to in the *Dhammalipi* very clearly. And the whole thing may be well summed up in the very words of the Emperer Asoka, that his people may trust him and grasp the truth that "the king is to us even as a father; he loves us even as he loves himself; we are to the king even as his children".[2]

This was in entire keeping with the duties of kings in ancient India, which was that between the king and the people, the duty was reciprocal. Kings had rights as well as duties; and that if he was, from one point of view, the master, from another he was the servant. The

1 *The Arthaśāstra*, Book, I. Chapter XIX.

2 Kaliṅga Edict. Principal Vidhusekhara Bhattacharyya in the *I. A.*, March, 1920, supporting Prof. Radhagovinda Basak doubts whether "the same daily routine was carried out in practice." He adduces in support of his theory that, "The fact, as has been related by Megasthenes, that Chandragupta used to receive petitions when he was being shampooed is no evidence that the was in the habit of acting upon the time-table enjoined in the *Arthaśāstra*."

king had to forego his own advantages for the general good. The *Sāstras* are very particular about it. The *Mahābhārata* lays down that the king who, taking the sixth part of the produce from his subjects, fails to protect them, is said to take upon himself the entire burden of their sins. *The Bhāgavāta Purāṇa* also echoes the same sentiment when it says, "Protection of his subjects is the highest of royal virtues by which in after life the king robs them of the sixth of their merits. Otherwise, by exacting taxes from his subjects and yet failing to protect them, he is robbed by his subjects of his merits and himself earns their sins." The *Mārkaṇdeya Purāṇa* also repeats the idea by thus observing, "If the subjects after paying a sixth of the produce as tribute to the king, have to be protected by another, the king is sure to go to hell ; this tribute has been fixed by former jurists as the king's salary for protecting his subjects ; if the king does not protect them in return, he robs them and is guilty of theft." The great writer on Hindu Polity in his *Arthaśāstra* also observed the same thing when he advised the king to devote only a part of his time in rest. Kauṭilya says, "The king shall divide both the day and the night into eight divisions. During the first one-eighth part of the day, he shall post watchmen and attend to the accounts of receipts and expenditure ; during the second part, he shall look to the affairs of both citizens and country and people. During the third, he shall not only bathe and dine, but also study ; during the fourth, he shall not only receive revenue in gold, but also attend to the appointments of superintendents ; during the fifth, he shall correspond in writs with the assembly of his ministers, and receive secret information gathered by his spies ; during the sixth he may engage himself in his favourite amusements or in self-deliberation ; during the seventh, he shall superintend elephants, horses, chariots and infantry ; and during the eighth part, he shall consider various plans of military preparation with his Commander-in-chief. At the close of the day, he shall observe the evening prayer.

"During the first one-eighth part of the night, he shall receive secret emissaries ; during the second he shall attend to baths, supper and study ; during the third, he shall enter the bed chamber and enjoy sleep during the fourth and fifth parts ; having been awakened by the sound of trumpets during the sixth part, he shall recall to his mind the injunctions of the Sciences as well as the day's duties ; during the seventh he shall sit considering administrative measures, and send out spies ; and during the eighth division of the night, he shall receive benedictions from sacrificial priests, teachers, and the high priest." That is to say, for only two hours and a half the king was to enjoy sleep—a very hard lot, indeed[1].

After having tried to throw light on some terms in the Edicts from the social and political points of view, I shall turn to discuss some terms bearing on the economic condition of India in the age of the Mauryas.

Economic aspects of the Edicts

The Superintendent of Pastures is referred to in Rock Edict XII. This officer was directly concerned with the sanctity of animal life, and there was some special reason for mentioning this officer. In this connection I like to refer to Rock Edict VI, where Asoka wanted to be informed of every thing at all times. There we find the term *Vachamhi* which has been translated into mews. That was one of the places which was frequently visited by the Emperor. And why ? The reason was this. *Vachamhi* is *Vraja*,[2] which means a herd of cattle, including cows, buffaloes, goats, sheep,

1 Shakespeare has observed very well—
"The King must guard that which he rules, and is but a hand,
To whom a space of land is given to plough,
Who may not wander from the allotted field
Before his work is done."

2 *The Arthaśāstra* II. 6. cf *I. A.*, XLVII, 1918 p., 53.

asses, camels, horses and mules. And we have to remember, in this connection, that very great attention was paid to the sanctity of animal life.

Pastures

Mr. V. A. Smith in referring to the former observes, "The king is bound to inspect his live stock"[1], but does not assign any reason for this. I venture to assign the following reason. In Rock Edict VI, the *Vraja* was one of the places frequented by the king, first because, as I think, the sanctity of animal life was one of the cardinal doctrines of the great Buddhist Emperor, and so his attention was naturally directed to the herds. And secondly, in those days very great attention was paid to cattle. There was, indeed, a register of cattle kept by the Superintendent of pastures. In it were noted the following varieties of cattle, *viz.*, male calves, steer, tameable draught oxen, bulls for impregnating the herd, oxen for pulling carts drawn by pairs, calves of which the flesh was food, buffaloes, female calves, heifers, young cows, pregnant cows, milch cows, cows and buffaloes that had not yet calved or were barren, male and female calves only a month or the old, or still younger. These together with the cattle that strayed and were not claimed for a month or two by the owner who lost them, were branded, and the Superintendent registered each of them according to its class as mentioned above, and also according to the brand, natural signs, colour and distance between the horns. The duty of the Superintendent was termed *Vraja Paryayam*. It was also the duty of the State to fix the scale and standard of diet normally necessary to keep up the health, vigour and working capacity of all live-stock. And it was also because of the importance which was paid to the live-stock that the Census of those days—a permanent institution of the Mauryas[2]—was instituted,

---

1 *Asoka*, p. 174.

2 *Vide* my *Lectures on the Economic Condition of Ancient India.*

when not only the total number of the inhabitants in each village was counted, but an account of the exact number of cultivators, cowherds, merchants, artisans, labourers, slaves, biped and quadruped animals also was kept.

Great attention was paid to agriculture in those days, and it was for this reason that the importance of livestock in India, pre-eminently an agricultural country, was fully realised even then, and special care was taken by Government for their healthy growth and improvement. There was arrangement for pastures and grazing grounds for the proper supply of fodder as well as for the welfare of live-stock in general, and there were no less than six officers for running the department. And hence, we find that the king was bound to inspect his live-stock.

Census

In this connection, it would not be out of place to refer here to the Census which, in those days, included not only the total number of the inhabitants of all the four castes in each village, but an account of the exact number of cultivators, cowherds, merchants, artisans, labourers, slaves, as well as an account of biped and quadruped animals. Indeed, the Census of the Mauryas was a permanent institution, not a periodical one, and it was a department of the State run by permanent officials. Census had already been in existence in several ancient countries of the world. The fighting strength of the children of Israel was ascertained at the Exodus. During the Babylonian captivity, a register of the population of each class was kept. For fixing the tribute, there was apparenly some method in force in Persia. Solon introduced an Egyptian ordinance in Athens which afterwards developed into an electoral record. In the Census introduced in Rome by Servius Tullius it was decreed that every fifth year the population should be enumerated along with the property of each family—land, live-stock, slaves and freedmen. But the Mauryan Census was superior to all these. It was a permanent institution, important from the political as well as from the economic standpoint. By such a Census, not only was the total number of inhabitants of all the four castes in each village known, but an account of the exact number of cultivators, cowherds, merchants, artisans, labourers, slaves, and biped and quadruped animals, fixing at the same time the amount of gold, free labour, and fines that could be collected from each house was also recorded.

Live-stock

Great attention was paid to agriculture and the Superintendent of Pastures referred to in Rock Edict XII and mentioned above, was an important officer, who has also been referred to in the *Arthaśāstra*. Importance of live-stock in India, pre-eminently a country of agriculture, was thus fully realised, and special care was taken by Government for their healthy growth and improvement. During the time of the Mauryas, there was a special department for pastures and grazing grounds, for the proper supply of fodder and for the welfare of live-stock in general and there were elaborate arrangements for running the department. It was, therefore, no wonder that the king himself was bound to inspect the live-stock, for, both from the religious as well as from the administrative points of view, it was imperatative.

The next question is an old one, and it arises in connection with our study of the celebrated Rummindeī Inscription on the pillar placed to commemorate the birth place of Buddha. "In as much as here the Holy one was born", the village of Lumbini was released from religious cesses and was required to pay (only) one-eighth as land revenue. The words used here are *Ubalikekaṭe*[1]. and *athabhagiyecha*. *Bali*, as explained by the *Arthaśāstra*,[2] was a special religious tax. It occurs several

1 Mr. V. A. Smith's translation.

2 II. 35.

times in the Rgveda in the sense of tribute to a King or offering to a God.[1] Exemption from this was granted to the villagers in commemoration of the king's visit to the sacred place. This is, of course, clear[2].

There is, however, some difficultiy about *athabhága*. *Bhága*, according to the *Arthaśástra*, means a portion of produce payable to the Government, but what was the share of the king? In Book II, chapter VI of the *Arthaśástra*, revenue from various sources are treated of. Produce from crown lands *(Sìta)*, portion of produce payable to the Government *(bhāga)*, religious taxes *(bali)*, taxes paid in money *(kara)*, merchants, the superintendents of rivers, ferries, boats and ships, towns, pasture-grounds, road-cess *(vartani)*, ropes *(rajju)* and ropes to bind thieves *(chorarajju)* come under the head of country parts. No mention is made here as to the amount of tax payable, but in the same book, chapter XXIV, we find the following: "Fields that are left unsown may be brought under cultivation by employing those who cultivate for half the share of the produce; or those who live by their own physical exertion may cultivate such fields for one-fourth or one-fifth of the produce grown; or they may pay (to the king) as much as they can without entaiing any hardship upon themselves". Here also we have no clear statement as to the revenue paid to the king. In another place Chánakya observes[3]: "In such parts of his countries as depend solely upon rain for water and are rich in grain, he may demand of his subjects one-third or one-fourth of their grain according to their capacity". In the same chapter we again find, "They were to pay one-fourths of their grain".

King's share

1 *Vedic Index*, II. 62.

2 Cf. *J. R. A. S.*, 1908, p. 850, note by Lyall, who holds that it was quit rent, as something less than the full assessment. Also, *Ibid*, 1909, p. 466, where Dr. Thomas explains the term as "free from taxes".

3 V. 2.

If we consult other authorities, we also find a good deal of variance. For example, Āpastamba says, "Land might be let against a half or other share of the produce."[1] Gautama says, "Cultivators must pay to the king a tax amounting to one-tenth, one-eighth or one-sixth of the produce."[2] Viṣṇu, on the other hand, maintains that only a sixth part of every kind of crop was to be paid, while a sixth, an eighth[3] or even a twelfth part of the crops is allowed by Manu. That great lawgiver observes, "As the leech, and calf, and the bee take their food little by little, even so must the king draw from his realm annual taxes. Of cattle, a fiftieth part may be taken by the king ; of grain an eighth, a sixth, or a twelfth according to the soil and the labour necessary to cultivate it"[4]. The *Mahābhārata*[5] allowed a sixth part, the *Mārkaṇḍeya Purāṇa* has also the same thing. The tax very likely varied under different circumstances, as is well stated by the *Śukranīti* : "The king should realise one-third, one-fourth or one-half from places which are irrigated by tanks, canals and wells, by rain and rivers, respectively"[6].

One-fourth was the proportion of the king's share as understood by Megasthenes. He observes that besides the land-tribute, the husbandman paid into the royal treasury a fourth part of the produce of the soil. Prof. Hopkins, however, is not prepared to accept what the Greeks said about the king's share. He says, "The fourth part, evidently declared by Megasthenes to be the proportion exacted, contradicts perpetual statement

---

1 II. 11. 28.

2 X. 24.

3 Chapter III.

4 VII. 129-132.

5 Śanti, LXXI.

6 IV. 2. 227. *The Śukranīti* I. 248 observes, as one of the duties of the king, "equitable realisation of revenue."

of native authorities that the proportion of grain is one-sixth and one-fourth in emergencies"[1].

Both Thomas and Smith, however have come to the conclusion that as *Saḍabhāga* in the *Arthaśāstra* is one-sixth,[2] *aṣṭabhāga* can mean only one-eighth and that the meaning is that the boon conferred on the people of Lumbini was that, instead of one-fourth, the revenue payable to the king as testified to by Megasthenes, the village had to pay one-eighth of its produce as land-revenue. That is to say, if Asoka was in the habit of taking one-fourth, the concession amounted to the remission of half the assessment[3]. But could not Asoka, a truly devout king, who could, as Hiuen Tsiang has observed, give away his kingdom thrice, forsake the one-eighth (as suggested), of the revenue of a small village? It was a very small matter to him and this interpretation, therefore, cannot be accepted. We would propose to adhere to the old interpretation which was that the village was made free of taxes and a recipient of wealth[4]. The fact that, according to the *Divyāvadāna*,[5] Asoka presented on his visit to Lumbini one hundred thousand *suvarṇas* to the people of the country, supports our contention.

Decline of Buddhism

A question which naturally strikes one is, how was it that in spite of the best efforts of Asoka, as shown particularly in his Edicts, Buddhism declined and Hinduism revived, and that even when the Mauryas were reigning in Magadha? Attempts have been made to

---

1 *Journal of the American Oriental Society*, XIII.

2 II. 12. Bühler took aṭha=*artha*—sharer in wealth, partaking of the king's bounty, but Pischel took aṭha=aṣṭa (with eight plots of assessable lands), a view accepted by Smith, but Fleet took it as paying an eighth share of the grain harvest, instead of a quarter share.

3 According to Fa-hien, the revenue was mainly derived from the rent of the crown lands, and the royal officers, being provided with fixed salaries had no occasion to live on the people.

4 *Epigraphia Indica*, v. 4.

5 P. 390.

answer this question by saying that it was the aggressive methods of Asoka to propagate the religion of the Buddha that brought about a reaction and the downfall of Buddhism. I am afraid this was not the real cause. We have already, as I venture to say, proved that so far as the propagation of Buddhism was concerned, there was nothing like coercion. Asoka, though keen about his *Dhamma*, was very tolerant and the traditions associated with his name as well as the orders inculcated through the medium of the Edicts go to prove definitely that he did not bear the least hatred towards Hinduism,[1] the religion which prevailed during the lifetime of his forefathers and which re-asserted itself soon after his death. His forwardness consisted in the inculcation of the sanctity of animal life—both by precepts as well as by examples, as it is manifest in the orders promulgated regarding the prohibition of killing animals for the royal kitchen—a measure which he was keen to introduce. This was one of his cardinal doctrines, and, if I may be permitted to say, this devotion to the sanctity of animal life to an inordinate degree was the main, at any rate, one of the main causes which brought about the downfall of the religion of Gautama Buddha. Asoka went too far for it and the result was the reaction against the sanctity of animal life. From the highest to the lowest, all turned against it. The revival of the *Aśvamedha* or the horse-sacrifice, by king Puṣyamitra[2] who brought about the downfall of the Maurya dynasty, and with it the renaissance of Hinduism, is a clear proof of what we venture to submit[3]. The result of Asoka's too strong a leaning towards the sanctity of animal life produced

1 M. M. H. P. Sâstri is against such a view. See his article, *Causes of the Dismemberment of the Maurya Empire*, *J. A. S. B.*, May 1910, pp 259 ff.

2 *Vide, ante*, p.—25.

3 "The sentiment in favour of respecting animal life, technically called the *ahimṣā* doctrine, had a large share in fixing on the necks of

a very marked reaction and this produced *pari passu* a feeling against the Buddhistic religion of Asoka. Instances of such occurrences are not rare in history. In the history of England, the austere Puritanism of Cromwell and his thousand and one regulations to support that, led to the reaction in the reign of Charles II. Here, also, we find the same thing. So far as theory was concerned, it was all very well to order that chaff must not be set on fire along with the living things in it,[1] or that on certain days of the first and second fortnights[2] horses were not to be branded, but it was practically impossible to observe them. Of course, so long as the strong hand of the Puritan King remained, these things were or might have been observed, but they could not continue for an indefinite time. Creed, social custom or religious sentiment, nothing could withstand the orders of the King, and the result was obvious. Capture or sale of fish for fifty-six days in the year, or similar prohibitions, must have been intolerably vexatious, and they must naturally and necessarily have caused hardship and trouble to the people who had been accustomed to look upon sacrifices as the way to salvation. In the hands of the Censors of the Law of Piety and their subordinates and underlings, we can presume that the royal orders must have created the worst possible troubles and anxieties, and naturally the people in general wanted to get rid of all

---

the people burdensome rules of conduct. That sentiment, which is known to have been actively encouraged by Jain and Buddhist teachers from about 500 B.C., probably originated at a much earlier date. The propagation of *ahiṃsā* necessarily produced a sharp conflict of ideas and principles of conduct between the adherents and the old-fashioned people who clung to bloody sacrifices, cow-killing and meat-eating. Communities which had renounced the old practices and condemned them as revolting impieties naturally separated themselves from their more easy-going and self-indulgent neighbours, and formed castes bound strongly to maintain the *novel* code of ethics". *The Oxford History of India*, page 38.

1 Pillar Edict, V.

2 *Ibid.*

these superfluous regulations regarding the sanctity of animal life. But Buddhism and animal sanctity had got intermingled together, more or less, inseparably, and the reaction against the one led to a revulsion of feeling against the other. The natural result was that while people got rid of the vexatious regulations regarding sacrifices and all these, they managed to throw Buddhism also into the background. Both had developed *pari passu* and with the wilhdrawal of the strongest Maurya hand, the regulations against *ahiṃsā* and the religion of the Tathāgata, both met with the same fate. Certainly it was not due merely to the aggression of Asoka.

Such was Asoka, the Imperial Saint, the great Maurya Emperor who raised the Land we live in to its climax of glory and position. From his Capital, of which I have already given you an account, he promulgated his regulations to make Buddhism his state religion and that of his neighbours as well. His last days were unpleasant; the accounts are conflicting, but if tradition is to be relied on, deprived of royalty and power, of health, of physique and of physicians, with no other support save that of the Buddhist *Saṃgha*, he made his last gift to it, the half of an *āmalaka* fruit, exemplifying the life which he had all along led and exclaiming with deep devotion and characteristic piety :—

" With faith unchangeable, which nought can shake
This gift of Earth's immeasurable sphere,
I to the Saints' Assembly freely make ;
And self-control I crave, of boons most dear,
A good which changeth never".

I hope you will now concur with me, even after this cursory analysis of the Edicts, that the general pervailing notion that the Edicts are merely of religious import, is not a very correct one and that they do throw a flood of light not only on the ethical aspect but also on the other mundane ones, *viz.*, social, political and economical, of the great Asoka of whom it has been so aptly said, "If a man's fame can be measured by the number of hearts who revere his memory, by the number of lips who have mentioned and still mention him with honour, Asoka is more famous than Charlemagne or Cæsar"[1].

1 Koppen.

NALANDA—GENERAL VIEW

To face p. 119.

COURTYARD OF MONASTERY AT NALANDA

To face p. 119.

LECTURE V

The University of Nalanda

The Site of Nālandā

The site of this widely known University of ancient India[1], which fulfilled the dictum of Carlyle that a true University is a collection of books, as well as that of Newman that it is a school of universal learning, implying the assemblage of strangers from all parts in one spot, the *alma mater* of a host of distinguished logicians, grammarians and philosophers, "the rendezvous of religious controversialists, the never-failing fountain-head from which Tibet and China imbibed a good deal of their learning and civilization," is indicated by the melancholy tanks and a long line of lofty mounds extending north and south for some 3,000 feet at Bargaon[2], at present a desolate, dust-covered hamlet, about eight miles from Rājgir. The place can be reached by the Bihar-Bakhtiarpur Light Railway station Nālandā, from which the ruins of the famous monastery can be seen and from which it is only a mile off. Scholars all over the world and we, the people of Bihar, are particularly

1 Besides the Nālandā, Vikramaśilā and Odandapuri Universities of Magadha, we had in ancient India the University of Taxilā, in the Punjab, the seat of a more or less Brāhmaṇical Institution, the University of Śrī Dhanya Kaṭaka on the banks of the Kṛṣṇā a seat of both Brāhmaṇical and Buddhistic learning Rai Bhahadur Saratchandra Das, relying on Tibetan accounts, is of opinion that the great monastery of Dapung in Tibet containing nearly 8,000 monks and a University with six colleges, was built after the model of the University of Śrī Dhanya Kaṭaka. Vide *Hindustan Review*, 1906.

2 Dr. Bloch in the *Journal of the Royal Asiatic Society*, 1909, p. 440, observes, "It is, perhaps, not generally known that the modern name of the site of Nālandā, is Baṛgar, not Bargaon, as Cunningham spelt it. I have had many occasions of hearing the name pronounced Baṛgar during my prolonged stay at Rajgir......Likewise I have no doubt that the modern name has been derived from a sacred *bar* tree (Sanskrit *Vaṭa, Ficus religiosa*) which has grown over one of the ruined brick buildings of ancient Nālandā."

grateful to the Royal Asiatic Society of Great Britain and Ireland for having made possible the excavation of this ancient and interesting site,[1] and we have no doubt that further traces of the big and impressive buildings described by the Chinese traveller, Hiuen Tsiang, will be discovered through the activities of the Archœological Department. General Cunningham, the father of Indian Archæology, who first truly identified the site, was quite correct when he observed that it possessed finer and more numerous specimens of sculpture than any other places he had visited. And considering the very large number of places which he had visited, many of which he had himself excavated, this may be considered as a high testimony[2].

Apart from the sculptures, some of which are even now available, we may also refer to the fine description of Hiuen Tsiang who says, "The richly adorned towers and the fairy-like turrets, like pointed hill-tops are congregated together. The observatories seem to be lost in the vapours (of the morning), and the upper rooms tower above the clouds. From the windows one may see how the winds and the clouds (produce new forms), and above the soaring eaves the conjunctions of the sun and the moon (may be observed). How the deep, translucent ponds bear on their surface the blue lotus, intermingled with the *Kaṇaka* flower of deep red colour ; and at intervals the *Āmra* groves spread their shade over all. All the outside courts, in which are the priests' chambers, are of four stages. The stages have dragon-projections and coloured eaves ; the pearl-red pillars, carved and

1 Dr. Spooner very aptly observed, "The Royal Asiatic Society's offer was peculiarly welcome to all concerned, the more so, since they very generously offered to present the Province with whatever might be found and the Local Government was good enough, despite the War to provide funds for the necessary acquisition of the land." *Annual Report of the Archæological Survey of India, Eastern Circle*, for 1915-1916, p. 34

2 "It is certainly a fact that a considerable portion of the finest sculptures in the Calcutta Museum originated from this very site." *Ibid*, p. 34.

ornamented, richly adorned balustrades, and roofs covered with tiles that reflect light in a thousand shades—these things add to the beauty of the scene"[1]. Besides the tanks, all that now remains of its splendid buildings, its spacious hall and dreaming spires, its long-extending corridors and splendid libraries, its incense-streaming temples and adjoining grounds is a heap of mounds which is now yielding a bumper harvest to the archæologists. In the words of one who has done so much to bring to the notice of the world the glorious sculptures and art of Magadha, but who has also done so much to injure it, "when the caves and temples of Rājgir were abandoned to ravages of decay and when the followers of Tathāgata forsook the mountain dwellings of their great teacher, the monastery of Nālandā arose in all its splendour on the banks of the lakes of Bargaon ; successive monarchs vied in its establishment ; lofty pagodas were raised in all directions, halls of disputation and schools of instruction were built between them ; shrines, temples and topes were constructed on the side of every tank and encircled the bases of every tower and around the whole mass of religious edifices were grouped the "four-storied dwellings of the preachers and teachers of Buddhism."[2] And recent excavations have shewn how the buildings were made of bricks of a superior quality and admirable texture—"fitted together so perfectly that in some places the joints between the bricks are altogether inconspicuous.[3]" As the late Dr. Spooner observed, "As brickwork the construction is remarkable, far superior to any modern work that I have seen in recent years."[4] This

1 *Life of Hiuen Tsiang*, p. 111.

2 Broadley : *Nālandā Monasteries at Bargaon. Sub-division Bihār, Zila Patna.*

3 *Archaeological Survey Reports, Eastern Circle*, 1915-16, pp. 115-118.

4 *Ibid.* Dr. Spooner has observed that, "It can now be demonstrated that upon this one spot four separate and successive monasteries have

testimony of an archælogist of the position and experience of Dr. Spooner is worth full consideration.

The Date of Nālandā

The year 450 is the earliest limit to which roughly can be assigned the royal recognition of Nālandā, though its early tradition betrays more or less a mythical character. Tāranāth would trace it to Asoka. He observes: "Here in Nālandā was in former times, the birthplace of the venerable Sāriputta and it is also the place where, he with 80,000 *arhats*, attained Nirvāṇa. In course of time, only the *Chaitya* of the venerable Sāriputta remained, at which King Asoka gave great offerings to the gods and to which he erected a great Buddhist temple...In this way the first founder of the Nālandā Vihār was Asoka." [1] But judging from the fact that there is no mention of it by Fa-hien, it would be very hard to accept this version of the Tibetan historian regarding the foundation of the University, though, presumably, the importance of the place reaches back to remote ages.

According to Hiuen Tsiang,[2] "not long after the Nirvāṇa of the Buddha, a former king[3] of this country, named Sakrāditya, built this Saṃghārāma. His son Buddhaguptarājā not only continued but added to it, while his son Tathāgataguptarājā followed in the footsteps of his father and grandfather. His successor Bālādityarājā added to the establishment, and his son Vajra also continued the pious object. Then a king of Central India emulated the example of these pious kings, by not only adding a new Saṃghārāma, but by building

---

been erected through a series of centuries, each being erected over the ruins of the previous one and the second in date enveloping the oldest." *Ibid*, 1916-17, p. 2.

1 Tāranāth also observes, p. 72, that a Brāhmaṇa Subiṣṇu, erected here 108 temples and also established 108 schools of *Abhidharma*. In one of the sculptures at Nālandā, Cunningham found inscribed *Āryya Sāriputta* and *Āryya Maudgalyāyana*.

2 *Records of Western Countries*, II, 168. In *The Life of Hiuen Tsiang*, we have "After the Nirvāṇa of Buddha." p. 40.

3 In the *Life*, we have "an old king".

round these edifices a high wall with one gate, which afterwards figured so prominently, being protected by the *Dvāra Paṇḍita*. Then followed a long succession of kings who continued the work of building, using all the skill of the sculptor till the whole became a truly marvellous sight."

Not only was it truly marvellous to the beholder, but its prosperity continued and I-Tsing who studied here for ten long years found it in a prosperous condition. Its name and fame flourished for long and in 750 the Tibetan king sent emissaries to Nālandā to invite its High Priest Kamalaśila[1] to confute heresies in his dominion and to bring about a renaissance of Buddhism. After this, its decadence commenced, very likely owing to the rise of the rival royal University of Vikramaśīlā, which became the premier educational establishment in Northern India. But as we read in the accounts relating to Vikramaśīlā, there was for some time an intercourse between the two Universities.[2] We have it also on record that the Tibetan monk who was sent by the king of Tibet to take Atiśa there from Vikramaśīlā stayed on his way at Nālandā.[3] And though Hiuen Tsiang mentioned a legend, that Nālandā was to be the model for a period of a thousand years[4], we may say that it did not retain its glory for so long a period.

According to Dr. Keilhorn, Buddhism was flourishing at Nālandā, as judged from the Ghosrawan inscription, which Major Kittoe, its discoverer, thought to have been inscribed between the middle of the ninth and tenth

---

1 Kamalaśila, flourished sometime between A. D. 728-776 and was a contemporary of Sānta Rakṣita who also went to Tibet. He specialised in *Tantra*.

2 Cf. Tāranāth, p. 236, where we are told of one āchāryya who was a gatekeeper both at Nālandā and Vikramāśilā. Cf. also, p. 250.

3 *Indian Pandits in the Land of Snow.*

4 Beal: *Records of Western Countries*, II, p. 170.

centuries.[1] This inscription, which I will refer to later on, was inscribed in the reign of Devapāla, and refers to the installation of a priest named Vīradeva as the superior priest at Nālandā. Mahāmahopādhyāya Haraprasād Sāstri is of opinion that, even during the tenth and eleventh centuries, Nālandā was a powerful rival of Vikramaśīlā, and Nālandā not only flourished but maintained its high position.[2] He supports this by mentioning that a manuscript copied at Nālandā in the sixth year of Mahipāla's reign[3] is to be found in the Library of the Asiatic Society. We shall presently speak of the various references to Nālandā, but we do not think we would be justified in coming to the conclusion that, even with the addition of some more references added to the one made by the learned scholar, Nālandā was in a very flourishing condition so late. Two causes must have contributed to its decay—its buildings must have become old and dilapidated owing to the lapse of ages and, secondly, it must have been cast into the shade by the growing splendours of the rival University of Vikramaśīla to which the attention of the kings was directed and which necessarily led to the withdrawal of royal patronage. The result was that the most remarkable *Saṃghārāma* languished. It did continue to exist however, even after the invasion of the Muhammedans, by whom it was destroyed along with the other Universities—for the *Pag-sam-jon-Zang* says that after the Muhammedan invasion the temples and *chaityas*

Causes of decay

1 *Vide J. A. S. B,* VII, Part I, 492-501 ; also Vol. XII, 268-274 ; also *Indian Antiquary,* XVII. 307-312. "Judging merely from the characters, the forms of which appear to me considerably earlier than those of an inscription of Mahipāla, I would assign it to the latter half of the 9th century ; while the latest researches by Dr. Hoernele on the chronology of the Pāla dynasty would rather bring it down about the middle of the tenth century. I do not think that the inscription can possibly be later." *I. A.,* 1888. Cf. Also *A. S. R.* Vol I, p. 38, Vol III. p. 120 and *Ancient Geography of India,* I. 44.

2 *Rāmacharita,* p. 12.

3 *Vide* Bendall's *Catalogue,* p. 101.

were repaired by a sage named Mudita Bhadra.[1] Soon after this, one Kukkuṭasidha, a minister of some king of Magadha, erected a temple at Nālandā, and while a religious sermon was being delivered there, two very indigent Tirthika mendicants appeared on the scene. Some wicked young novice-monks threw dirty water on them in disdain. This made the mendicants very angry. After propitiating the sun for twelve years, they performed a fire-sacrifice and threw living embers and ashes from the sacrificial pit into the Buddhist temples. This destroyed completely not only the fine library, but the buildings too. That the buildings were destroyed by fire is evidenced by the Bālāditya inscription,[2] which also we shall refer to later on.

Whatever may be the exact date of the establishment of the University of Nālandā, the place was an important one even in the days of the Buddha. He stayed for some time at Nālandā where he went with a great company of the brethren and stopped at the Pāvārika Mango-grove. He was met here by the venerable Sāriputta and solved that disciple's difficulties. Here also he had that comprehensive religious talk with the *Saṃgha* on the nature of upright conduct, of earnest contemplation and of intelligence.[3] One of Nālandā's villagers named Lepa has been described as prosperous, famous, rich in high and large houses, beds, seats, vehicles, and chariots, abounding in riches, gold and silver, possessed of useful and necessary things, owning many male and female slaves, cows, buffaloes, and sheep. Buddha spent some time in one of the bathing halls of this rich Lepa, where Udaka came, heard a long discourse

Mention of Nālandā

Antiquity of Nālandā

1 *Indian Logic—Mediæval School*, p. 147. 'The Turks, conquered the whole of Magadha and destroyed many Vihāras; also in Srī-Nālandā much damage was done and the priests fled abroad." Tāranāth, p. 94.

2 *Archæological Survey Report*, III. 122. *Journal and Proceedings of the Asiatic Society of Bengal*, IV. 105.

3 *Mahāparinibbāna-Sutta.*

from him and was converted. From Nālandā the Great One went to Pāṭaliputra which was evidently inferior to the former in the eyes of Ānanda who did not consider Pāṭaliputra to be a fit place for the Buddha's Nirvāna, while Nālandā was considered fit. That would evidently show that so far as importance went, Nālandā was superior to Pāṭaliputra and it may be, therefore, taken for granted that Nālanda was also older than Pāṭaliputra. The *Kalpasūtra* mentions that the other great religious leader and teacher, Mahāvīra, also spent some time here. In the *Sutrakritaṅga*, Nālandā is described as containing many hundreds of buildings, though it was then only a suburb of Rājagṛha.

In the *Dighha Nikāya* we find mentioned the name of the village Nālandā, near Rājagṛha, with a Pāvārika Mango Park, and Āmra seems to have been the name of the original owner of the site of the Nālandā establishment. Here we find that a young householder tried to induce the Tathāgata to exibit miraculous powers saying, "This Nālandā of ours, Sir, is influential and prosperous, full of folk, crowded with people, devoted to the Blessed One. It were well, if the Exalted One were to give command to some brother to perform by powers surpassing those of an ordinary man a mystic miracle." Needless to say, the great Tathāgata spoke against the use of miraculous powers. There is also mentioned a Rest House called *Āmravātika* where Buddha spent a night.

Description by Hiuen Tsiang

Coming to the Chinese travellers, Fa-hien does not mention Nālandā[1]. He mentions the name of a village called Nālo which some archæologists have tried to identify as Nālandā, but this identification has not been and cannot be accepted. We are sure that if Nālandā was at the time of the visit of Fa-hien worth visiting, he would not have left it undescribed.[2] That evidently

1 See Cunnigham, *Archaeological Survey Report*, 1861-62.

2 See *Travels of Fa-hien*, Beal's Edition.

shows that the *Saṃghārāma* did not exist then, or, at any rate had not acquired any celebrity whatever to attract the foreign seeker after truth. It is Hiuen Tsiang who has given us a full description of the Nālandā establishment and University, "where students from all over India came together from the distance of 10,000 li,"[1] and where "priests or strangers always reach to the number of 10,000,"[2] and of its monasteries and their builders, the teachers and the taught. "The priests to the number of several thousands, are men of the highest ability and talent."[3] That prince of travellers continues: "Their distinction is very great at the present time, and there are many hundreds whose fame has rapidly spread through distant regions. Their conduct is pure and unblamable. They follow in sincerity the precepts of the moral law. The rules of this convent are severe and all the priests are bound to observe them. The countries of India respect them and follow them. The day is not sufficient for asking and answering questions".[4] Such was the value of the hall-mark of the University that we find that persons wanted to "usurp" the name of the Nālandā students, in order to receive honour in consequence. So high was the standard, that those desirous of entering the University and taking part in the discussion, had first to engage in disputation with the *Dvāra Paṇḍita* (the keeper at the gate), who proposed such hard questions that "those who fail compared with those who succeed are as seven or eight to ten." And even the two or three who succeeded in defeating the gate keeper were invariably humbled in the assembly. Evidently that showed the high standard of the *alumni* of the Nālandā

1 Beal, Vol. II, p. 169.

2 *The Life of Hiuen Tsiang*, p. 112.

3 *Records of Western Countries*, Vol. II, 170.

4 *Ibid*, p. 171.

University which concerned itself with what we would call higher teaching, the examination at the gate being the Matriculation of the scholars to enable them to enter the portals of the University.

The fine description of Hiuen Tsiang has been supplemented by I—Tsing who has given us the fullest details in his *Buddhist Practices in India*, of the curriculum of studies and the method of the observances of religious rites at Nālandā. This scholar started from China in 671, and arrived at Tāmralipti, the modern Tamluk, in Bengal, in 673. He studied at Nālandā for a considerable time and collected some four hundred Sanskrit Texts, amounting to 5,00,000 slokas. During his time, there were eight halls and three hundred appartments.

Nālandā is also mentioned in connection with the names of a number of Chinese travellers, who came to India with the object of studying at the famous University [1].

1—i The Sramaṇa Hiuen Chin, known as Prakāsmati, came to Nālandā in the seventh century and remained there for three years.

ii Taou-hi, known as Srīdeva, dwelt at the Nālandā monastery where he studied the Mahāyāna.

iii Āryavarmana a Corean monk, died at Nālandā after stopping there for some time.

iv Another Corean monk reached Nālandā in 688 for studying.

v Tchehong came in the 7th century and remained at Nālandā for eight years.

vi Onkong, known as Dharmadhātu, studied at Nālandā for three years.

vii I-Tsing mentions Buddha-Karma whom he met at Nālandā.

viii Tao-Fang, known as Chandradeva, also visited it.

ix Tang Tang, a priest belonging to the Mahāyāna school, also visited Nālandā

x A Corean monk, named Hwin Sun, better known as Prayānavarmā, visited Nālandā.

xi A priest of King-Chau, known as Silaprabhā, studied the *Kośa* here.

xii Hiuen Tata studied at the University for ten years.

xiii Won-Hing, known as Prāgñadeva, studied the *Koṣa* here.

Besides the above, both Hiuen Tsiang and I-Tsing mention Jñānchandra (*Memoirs*, IX. 47). Another, Ratnasiṃha is mentioned. (General Introduction, (viii), *A Record of the Buddhist Religion*.)

Two Tibetan traditions mention Nālandā, one before the days of Nāgārjuna, of whom we shall speak later on, and the other also in conection with that great scholar when one of his contemporaries, a Brāhmaṇa, named Subiṣṇu established one hundred and eight temples at Nālandā [1].

We may here refer to various epigraphic and other references in connection with Nālandā.

References to Nālandā

I. In the beginning of the eighth century A. D.,[2] two eminent teachers from Magadha visited Tibet at the invitation of King Thisong-den-tsan and formally introduced the religion of the Buddha there. S'ānta Rakṣita, who was at that time the High Priest of the monastery of Nālandā, was invited by the Tibetan king. He was received by the Tibetans with all the honours due to his high position as the spiritual teacher of the king of Magadha and was given the title of Āchāryya Bodhisattva. He was appointed High Priest of Tibet, and under his direction was introduced, for the first time, the system of Buddhist monachism now known as Lamaism in Tibet. At this time a Chinese missionary named Hosang Mahāyāna visited Tibet and as Hosang was superior to S'ānta, the king sent for the Buddhist philosopher Kamala S'īla of Magadha, who visited Tibet, defeated Hosang in the presence of the assembled court and was placed at the head of the metaphysical branch of the Buddhist church in Tibet.[3]

II. In the reign of Devapāla, of the Pāla dynasty, Nālandā was visited by Vīradeva, an inhabitant of

---

1 S. C. Vidyābhūṣaṇa's *Mediæval Logic.* Vide also Tāranāth, quoted *ante.*

2 According to Dr. Levi Buddhism was *introduced* into Tibet in the seventh century. He observes in *Ancient India* : " In the seventh century Indian Buddhism conquers yet another field for Indian culture : in the high lands of Tibet a rude and barbarous population sees monasteries rise where zealous missionaries translate from the Sanskrit the enormous mass of the canonical texts."

3 S. C. Dass, *Indian Pandits in the land of Snow.*

Nagarhara, and Devapāla made him the high priest [1].

III. Paṇḍita Hirananda S'astri, who was for some time in charge of the Nālandā excavations, [2] discovered a record inscribed on both sides, of a large copper plate surmounted by a seal soldered to its top, bearing an emblem, the *Dharmachakra*, flanked by two gazelles, the insignia of Nālandā. It had suffered in the fire which had destroyed the building. The seal bears the legend " S'rī-Devapāla Devasya, " *i. e.*, of Devapāladeva, who, as already noted, was the third sovereign of the Pāla dynasty. This record tells us of the grant of certain villages in the Rājagṛha and Gayā districts of the S'rī-nagara, identified with Pāṭaliputra division, for the upkeep of the monastery at Nālandā, and for the comfort of Bhikṣus coming there from the four quarters, for medical aid, for the writing of *Dharma Ratṇas*, or religious books [3], and for similar purposes.

IV. In the *Journal of the Bihar and Orissa Research Society*, (X. 37), Professor S. N. Majumder S'āstri gives us

1 For the Devapāla Inscription, *Vide Asiatic Researches* I. 123 and *Indian Antiquary*, XXI. This inscription of Devapāla, being a grant from Monghyr, was discovered in 1780. For many of these inscriptions *Gauḍa Lekhamālā* is invaluable. For this inscription, *Vīradeva-Prasasti*, *Vide J. A. S. B.*, Vol. XVII, Part I. Also *Indian Antiquary*, Vol. XVII, pp. 307-312. In this inscription occurs *Nālandā paripālanaya*. Dr. Hultzsch referring to this says, Satyabādi may have been Vīradeva's predecessor in Nālandā. Mr. Akṣay Kumar Maitreya suggests that very likely it referred to the Bodhi tree. *Cf. Gauḍa Lekhamālā*.

2 There is a sort of " post-script " in this, " which glorifies the ambassador, Balavarmma, and his liege-lord Srī Balaputradeva, the king of Suvarṇadvīpa." Pt. Hirānanda Sāstri wants to identify the Suvarṇadvīpa with the modern Sumatra. *The Annual Report of the Archæological Survey Report of India* backed this identification by the fact that Balaputradeva has been described as the grandson of the king of *Yubabhūmi*, which is evidently Java. *A. S. R.* 1920-21, *p.* 27. The inscription has been edited by the learned Paṇḍita in *Epigraphia Indica*, XVII. Lines 1-25 have been also translated in the Monghyr grant edited by Keilhorn in *the Indian Antiquary*, XXI, p p. 257-258.

3 In those times scholars after finishing their student-lives devoted themselves to the study of their sacred books in monasteries, when copying the manuscripts was considered a part of their duty.

Hilsa Statue

To face p. 131.

interesting facts regarding the Hilsā statue inscription of the thirty-fifth year of Devapāla which recorded the installation by Gaṇgādhara. The importance of this lies in the fact that this record extends the reign of Devapāla by two years and Mr. S'āstri concludes that it is the *earliest* Buddhist statue of the Pāla period for the " latest recorded regnal year for Devapāla was 33 as supplied by his Monghyr Grant". Further, it is the earliest Buddhist statute—Tārā of the Pāla period, which, not only mentions Nālandā and its famous Buddhist convent, but it also mentions a learned scholar Mañjusrīdeva, whose date is thus made clear.

V. In 1862, Cunningham brought to the notice of the public, the existence of an inscription at the foot of a sculpture, Vāgìṣvarī, at Nālandā[2]. As it is inscribed on the idol Vāgìṣvarī, it is known as Vāgiṣvarī inscription. It was discovered by Buchanan Hamilton and it figures in Martin's *Eastern India*[3]. The inscription records the name of *Paramabhaṭṭāraka Mahārājādhirāja* S'rì Gopāla at Nālandā[4].

VI. In the fifth regnal year of Mahipāla was copied at Nālandā *Aṣṭa Sāhasrika Prajñāpāramitā* which is now preserved in the library at Cambridge[5].

VII. In the sixth regnal year of the same sovereign an *Aṣṭasāhasrikā Prajñāpāramitā* was copied by Kalyānamitra Chintāmani at Nālandā, at the expense of *Sthavira* Sādhugupta of Tāribāri Mahāvihāra. This fine manuscript was discovered by Mahāmahopādhyāya Haraprasad

1 According to Paṇḍita Hīrānanda Śāstrī, the epigraph of the grant shows that King Devapāladeva granted these villages and apparently built this monastery of Nālandā at the instance of the King of Sumatra.

2 *Archæological Survey Report*, I. I.

3 I. Plate XV.

4 *Vide Gauḍa Lekhamālā*, pp. 86 and 87. Also *J. A. S. B.*, 1908, p. 105. The last word of this inscription was read by M. M. H. P. Sastri as Suvarṇa Vṛhisakta.

5 Bendall's *Catalogue*.

Sāstrī in Nepal and is now preserved in the Library of the Asiatic Society of Bengal. Mahipāla has been described as *Paramabhāṭṭāraka Mahārajādhirāja Parameśvara Paramasaugata.*[1].

VIII. In 1864 was discovered, among the ruins at Nālandā by Captain Marshall, [2] an inscription, since known as the Bālāditya inscription, preserved now in the Calcutta Museum. In it we find a reference to the rebuilding of a temple after its destruction by fire.

IX. In the reign of Nayāpāla, who died in 1045, Dvīpankara S'rījñāna was at the head of the University and he went to Tibet at the request of the king of Tibet[3].

X. In the fourth regnal year of Rāmapāla, one Grahṇakuṇdu copied an *Aṣṭasāhasrikā Prajñāpāramitā.* The writer, as it appears from the fly-leaf, was then at Nālandā, and Rāmpāla is described as *Mahārājādhirāja Parameśvara Paramasaugata*[4].

XI. In 1165 was copied an *Aṣṭasāhasrikā Prajnāpāramitā* at Nālandā, which is now in the library of the Royal Asiatic Society of Great Britain and Ireland[5]. From the *puṣpika* (colophon) we find that Nālandā's king was then *Parameśvara Paramabhaṭṭāraka Paramasaugata Mahārājādhirāja* Srimad Govindapāla. The copy was made, as we learn from the same colophon, in Govindapāla's fourth regnal year.

XII. The Royal Asiatic Society's excavations at Nālandā have also brought out a coin of Govinda Chandra[6].

---

1 *Proceedings of the Asiatic Society of Bengal*, 1809, p. 69.

2 *A. S. R.*, III, 122; *Journal and Proceedings, A. S. B.*, IV. (N. S.), 106.

3 *Indian Pandits in the Land of Snow*, p. 51 ff.

4 *Catalogue of Sanskrit Manuscripts in the Bodelian Library*, Cambridge, Vol. II. p. 250.

5 *J. R. A. S.*, New Series, VII, 1876, p. 3.

6 *Annual Report of the Archæological Survey of India, Eastern Circle* 1916-17, p. 41.

XIII. I may be permitted to mention also the discovery of seals, "Śri Nālandā-Mahāvihāriya Ārya-Bhikṣu-Saṃghasya" or the Venerable Community of Monks in the great Vihār of Śrì Nālandā[1].

IV. And lastly, an undated inscription has been discovered at Benares, which Dr. Vogel thinks to be of the eighth or ninth century, in which there is a reference to a pious gift at the glorious Nālandā[2] by Dandika, an inhabitant of Araṇyagiri belonging to the district of Nālandā.

Hiuen Tsiang, to whom we are so much indebted for the description of Nālandā observes thus about the name of the place : "The old accounts of the country say that to the south of the *Saṃghārāma* in the middle of an *Āmra* grove, there is a tank. The Nāga of this tank is called Nālandā. But the truth is, that Tathāgata in old days practised the life of a Bodhisattva here, became the king of a great country and established his capital in this land. Moved by pity for living things, he delighted in continually relieving them. In remembrance of this virtue, he was called 'charity without intermission'—*Nā-ālam-dā*—and the *Saṃghārāma* was so called in perpetuation of his name."[3] According to the other Chinese traveller, I-Tsing, the name Nālandā was derived from the name of Nāga Nanda[4]. General Cunningham, to whom we all are so indebted, accepted this and observed that to the south of the monastery there was a Nāga[5] or

1 *Ibid*, p. 43. The seal consists of the Wheel of Law flanked by two gazelles, recumbent with heads upraised, looking towards the Wheel. " This is the most interesting feature of these seals, because it shows that the venerable community of monks at Srī Nālandā copied on their seals the insignia of the monastery at Sārnāth." Why Nālandā should have copied it, is not known.

2 *Archaelogical Survey Reports*. 1903-4, p. 219 and 226. *Cf.* also Cunningham, *A. S. R.*, Vol. I, plate XIII, 2.

3 *Buddhist Records of the Western World*, II. 167.

4 Dr. Takakusu's edition. Tāranāth speaks of a Nāga (p. 39) in connexion with Pāṭaliputra also.

5 *A. S. R.* I.

dragon, Nālandā, and the place was named after him. In two inscriptions, which he discovered there, he found the name as Nālandā. No other theory has been suggested about the name.

The date of Nālandā

We have already observed that Fa-hien who came to India in or about 400 A. D., does not mention Nālandā. He speaks of the village of Nālo, which some scholars[1] have identified with Nālandā. But this identification cannot hold good. As we have suggested before, very likely the University did not exist then, or, at any rate, had not attained any significance to draw the attention of the traveller. Early in the seventh century, Hiuen Tsiang came to India, halted at Nālandā for the pretty long period of nineteen months to study. According to him, the site of Nālandā was originally a mango garden which was bought by five hundred merchants at a cost of ten *koṭis* of gold pieces and given to the Buddha to enable the merchants to obtain the fruit of holiness. There is, however, no reference to this, and scholars have come to the conclusion that it must have been given to a Buddhist saint of a later age and not to the Buddha himself[2].

Hiuen Tsiang further observes that after[3] the Nirvāna of the Buddha five kings named Sakrāditya, Buddhagupta, Tathāgata, Bālāditya and Vajra built five *Saṃghārāmas*. A king of Central India,[4] whose name Hiuen

1 Fa-hien, Legge's edition, *Buddhist Records of the Western World*, I. LVIII.

2 *Indian Logic : Mediæval School*, by M. M. S. C. Vidyabhusana, p. 145.

3 There is a slight difference here, which we have already noted, *viz.*, the *Records* say, "not long after the Nirvāṇa of Buddha," while the *Life* says "After the Nirvāṇa." *Vide* the Footnote on p. 112 of the *Life Hiuen Tsiang* regarding the question of date.

4 A fine bronze (or copper ?) pillar has been discovered at Nālandā. With reference to this Dr. Spooner observes : "This pillar is unique in my experience. It stands over four feet in height. The lower half is plain, but the upper is fashioned into a sort of capital, showing the form of a recumbent elephant surmounted by a maned lion, upon whose head

Tsiang does not mention, established another magnificent monastery, and he built round these edifices a high wall with one gate, probably the one mentioned by Hiuen Tsiang himself, where the *Dvāra Paṇḍita* sat and tested the fitness of outsiders to join in the disputations. Then we know from the same authority, a fact which we have already referred to, that a succession of kings continued to improve the buildings, using all the skill of the sculptor, till they were marvellous structures.

Bālāditya[1] the king of Magadha, who built one of the monasteries at Nālandā was a contemporary of the Hun King, Mihirakula[2]. Mihirakula began his reign in 515, and, therefore, his contemporary Bālāditya must have also lived about this time. Bālāditya, and three of his predecessors had also built monasteries. If we take 25 years as the average of each reign, Sakrāditya can be said to have reigned about 450 A. D[3]. The date of the temple may be, therefore, about 450.

General Cunningham came to the following conclusion. He observes : "The great monastery itself can be readily traced by the square patches of cultivation amongst a long mass of brick ruins 1,600 feet by 400 feet. These

---

rest two horizontal discs capped by a lotus-bud. What Hsian Chuang tells us of one of the great monasteries here at Nālandā having been built by a king of " Central India " might tempt one to wonder whether there is any connection between his account and this representation of the emblem of the Gond Kings of the Central Provinces". *Annual Report of the Archæological Survey of India*, Eastern Circle, 1916-17, p. 42.

1 Dr. Takakusu, the learned translator of I-Tsing's book, was of opinion that Bālāditya came to the throne in 481. *Vide Journal of the Royal Asiatic Society*, 1905. This opinion has not been generally accepted,

2 *Vide* Watters, *Yuan Chuang*. I. 289. Cf. also the *Early History of India*, p. 316, where V. A. Smith assigns 510 as the probable date of the accession of Mihirkula.

3 One of the Corean travellers says that the Nālandā temple was built by an old king named S'rī Sakrāditya for a Bhikṣu of Northern India. After beginning it, the king was much obstructed, and his descendants finished it. It was made the most magnificent establishment in *Jambudvīpa.*

open spaces show the position of the courtyards of the six smaller monasteries which are described by Hiuen Tsiang as being situated within one enclosure forming altogether eight courts. Five of the monasteries were built by five consecutive princes of the same family and the sixth by their successor called the king of Central India. No dates are given, but from the total silence of Fa-hien regarding any of the magnificent buildings at Nālandā, which are so minutely described by Hiuen Tsiang, I infer that they must have been built after 410. Surely, if the lofty temple of King Bālāditya which was 300 feet in height had then existed, it seems scarcely possible that Fa-hien should not have noticed it. I would, therefore, assign the probable date of the temple and monasteris of Nālandā to the two centuries between the visits of Fa-hien and Hiuen Tsiang, or from A. D. 425 to 625."[1]

There is another point which may as well be considered in this connection. Hiuen Tsiang records that the great temple of Bālāditya was similar to that of the temple at Buddha Gaya. As similarity of style may be taken as denoting proximity of date, the erection of Bālāditya's temple may, with great probability, be assigned to the same century in which the Vajrāsana temple was built. The date of the Nālandā temple may, therefore, be between 450 and 550 A. D.

It may be here mentioned that the views expressed by Dr. Cunningham about the date of the building of the temple is based on the theory that it was built at the time when the Budha Gaya one was built, will naturally fall to the ground, if we are to accept the view that the Vajrāsana temple was built during the time of the Kuṣān dynasty. This theory has been supported by the discovery of a terra-cotta plaque, by Dr. D. B.

1 *Archaeological Survey Report*, Vol. I, p. 29.

THE TEMPLE AT BUDDHA GAYA
(Before repairs)

To face p. 136.

The Temple at Buddha Gaya.

Spooner during his excavations at Pāṭaliputra[1]. This plaque bears the illustration of a temple, which Dr. Spooner supposed to be that of the original temple of Buddha Gaya and it also contains some characters in Kharosthi; and considering that the Kharosthi script was introduced into India in the second century A. D., it may be surmised that the temple was built during the Kuśān time. That would place the building of the temple very early, but a consideration of other circumstances, specially the fact that Nālandā was not at all mentioned by Fa-hien, leads one to reject this theory and to accept Cunningham's. *But no definite conclusion can be arrived at unless there are thorough excavations of the sites, and until we see the actual plinth of the temple itself, it would be hazardous to come to a definite conclusion.*

Endowments to the University

We have already referred to the rich endowments made to the University. Indeed, successive kings vied with one another in this respect. When Hiuen Tsiang was there, he found that the king of the country respected and honoured the priests, and the revenue of about one hundred villages went to the endowment of the University. Two hundred householders of these villages, day by day, contributed several hundred piculs[2] of ordinary rice and seven hundred catties[3] in weight of milk and butter. Hence, the students being so abundantly supplied, did not require to beg for their requisites[4]. Hiuen Tsiang was given every day 120 *jambiras*, 20 *pugas*[5] and a peck of *Mahāsāli* rice[6]. Every month he was also presented

1 *Annual Report of the Archæological Survey, Eastern Circle*, 1913-14, p. 71. *Cf.* also in *the Journal of the Royal Asiatic Society*, 1915, Dr. Spooner's article on the same subject.

2 I picul...138, 1/8 lbs.

3 I catty...160 lbs.

4 *The Life of Hiuen Tsiang*, p. 113.

5 Areca nuts.

6 "The rice was as large as the black bean and when cooked was aromatic and shining like no other rice at all." *The Life of Hiuen Tsiang*, p. 108.

with three measures of oil, a supply of butter and other things according to his needs.

The other traveller, I-Tsing, referring to the endowments to the University, observed that the lands in its possession contained more than two hundred villages, thus showing that, from the time of the visit of Hieun Tsiang to I-Tsing's time, the revenue of another hundred villages was placed at the disposal of the University, testifying that it was at the highest pinnacle of its glory. These villages, as attested by the scholar, were bestowed upon the monastery by kings of many generations.[1] Evidently, the result was the continuation of the prosperity of the University.

We have already referred twice to the rigid test for admission into the University, and we need not revert to it. Teaching was both tutorial and professorial and there was close touch between the professors and the students. As we find in I-Tsing, the old idea of serving the teacher pervaded the establishment, and the spirit of the Hindu times continued in these days also and existed in these Buddhistic extablishments, that is to say, the relationship was mutual. After graduation, the students proceeded to the king's court for appointment to the public services.[2] In Hiuen Tsiang's time ten thousand students studied the Greater Vehicle[3] and also the works belonging to the eighteen schools of Buddhism. But

Teaching & Curriculum

---

1 Takakusu's edition, p. 56.

2 *Life of Hiuen Tsiang*, p. 112.

3 The Mahayanist and the Hinayanist differ on the question of the divinity of the Buddha, the former looking upon the Buddha as a divinity and as such an eternal being coming to earth only for the salvation or deliverence of the being tortured by Māra, while the latter considers him as the Projenitor of the Law, regarding him as a "Super-man", believeing in the Triad and worshipping it in the order of Buddha, Dharma and Saṃgha—the Promulgator of the Law first, the Law being considered as the second, the third being the recipients of the Law. In the Mahāyāna, the order becomes Dharma, Buddha and Saṃgha, Buddha becoming only the *upāya* or the means of obtaining the knowledge which is diffused into the masses through him. For details, see B. C. Bhattacharyya's *Buddhist Iconography*.

that was not all, for that would show that the teaching was only secular. It was not really secular, for even ordinary works such as the Vedas and other books, *Hetuvidyā*, *Sabdavidyā*, *Chikitsāvidyā* (the science of healing), the works on *Tantra*[1] (Magic) and the *Sāṃkhya* were studied. In addition to all these, we find that the students investigated "miscellaneous works," whatever that phrase may mean. The result was that there was one thousand men who could explain the collection of sūtras and śāstras ; five hundred who could explain thirty collections and there were ten men, including the Master of the Law (we can take him to be the Vice-Chancellor in our modern parlance), who could explain fifty collections. There were one hundred pulpits, whence the teachers discoursed on their subjects. The prominent teachers then were Dharmapāla[2] who was abbot for a long time and Chandrapāla, Guṇamati and Sthiramati, Prabhāmitra and Jinamitra author of the *Mūla Sarvāstivāda Nikāya*, Jñānachandra and S'īlabhadra, the last being the head of the establishment. He was a prince of Bengal but had renounced the world, and he alone could explain the entire collection of sūtras and śāstras. It was under this eminent, virtuous and aged logician and master of the *śāstras*, that Hiuen Tsiang studied. Needless to say that, in addition to all these, there were many more of rare ability and talent, whose distinction was very great, and there were undoubtedly many hundreds whose fame spread to distant regions, and thereby attracted students to the great University.

---

1 According to Mahāmahopādhyaya H. P. Sāstri, "Tantra is very loosely used. Ordinary people understand it ,by any system other than the Vedas. But it realy means the workship of Sakti or female energy. The female energy is worshipped in conjunction with the male and the female energy is the essence of Tantra." Introduction to *Modern Buddhism*, p. 10.

2 Both Hiuen Tsiang and I-Tsing mention him, the former speaking of him as one of the great Bodhisattvas who rendered great service to Buddhism. *Buddhist Records of the Western World*, I.

Of the scholars mentioned by I-Tsing,[1] *viz.*, Nāgārjuna, Deva, Aśvaghoṣa, Vasu Vandhu, Asaṇga, Dignāga, Kamalaśila,[2] Saṃghabhadra and others,[3] who went to Tibet at the invitation of its king, Nāgārjuna stands supreme. We have no authentic record of the life of this scholar, but for all general purposes, the following, though more or less legendary, may be given[4]. A rich Brāhmaṇa of Vidarva, to whom no son had been born for many years, once saw in a vision that if he gave alms to one hundred Brāhmaṇas, he would get a son. He did so accordingly, and a son was born, but the astrologers predicted that the child would not live for more than a week. They were, therefore, requested to find a remedy for averting such a calamity and they asserted that his life could be prolonged for seven years only if the parents entertained one hundred Bhikṣus. Of course, this was done, and the child lived on until the fatal seventh year began when his parents, unwilling to see the painful end, caused him to be removed to a solitary place in company with a few retainers. As the boy was passing his last mournful days, one day the Mahābodhisattva Avalokiteśvara visited him in disguise and advised him to go to the great monastery of Nālandā as the surest means of escaping from the hands of death. The boy, accordingly, repaired thither and informed the head of the monastery of his impending danger. The

Nāgārjuna

1 He mentions Nāgārjuna first, then Deva and Aśvaghoṣa As a patriarch of northern Buddhism, Aśvaghoṣa has an earlier place than the rest, the former being the twelfth and the latter the fourteenth patriarch.

2 The *Tattvasaṃgraha* of Sāntarakṣita with the commentary or *Pañjika* of Kamalaśīla has been ably edited by Mr. B. C. Bhattacharyya in the Gaekwaḍ Oriental Series.

3 *Cf.* page 181 of *A Record of the Buddhist Religion* and the footnote on the same page by Dr. Takakusu.

4 *Indian Antiquary*, July 1908. *Cf.* Also *Journal of the Asiatic Society of Bengal*, LI, pp. 115 ff. "The extant accounts of Nāgārjuna are too legendary to permit of historical deductions." *Hinduism and Buddhism*, p. xxxii.

latter, thereupon, advised him to enter the holy order of monks. This saved him from the clutches of death, and he was ordained a Bhikṣu and commenced his studies there. After a few years' service in the monastery, he obtained the subordinate office of steward of the congregation. During the first part of the tenure of that office, Nāgārjuna propitiated the goddess Chaṇdikā, by whose agency he succeeded in providing the great body of the priests with the necessaries of life. He learnt many other mystic arts and by his religious practices he obtained the perfection of *siddhi*, *i. e.* success. Even the Nāgās used to attend his sermons in the shape of young boys, and they invited him to their abode in the land of the Nāgās where he spent three months. He was asked to settle permanently there, but he declined on the ground of his being required to preach the sacred religion in Jambudvīpa. He returned to Nālandā with costly presents and also with a religious book called *Nāga Sahasrika*. It was for this connection with the Nāgās that he obtained the name of Nāgārjuna. He afterwards visited many holy places and then returned to his own country where he erected many *chaityas* and composed many works on Science, Medicine, Astronomy and Alchemy. When the high priest of Nālandā died, Nāgārjuna succeeded him and matured the *Madhyamika* philosophy, which had been conceived by his illustrious teacher and predecessor. He finally became the head of the whole Buddhistic Church. It is said that Nāgārjuna will re-appear in India and live for full one hundred years to teach again the sacred *Dhamma* of the Law of Buddha[1].

1 Watters considers that Nāgārjuna probably lived about the 3rd century A. D., and the general testimony as to his native place is that he was born in Vidarva. (*I. A.*, 1908, p. 2c6). "Nāgārjuna, the founder of the Mādhyantikā philosophy, appears in literature as a man of remarkable genius, as an universal scholar, a Buddhist religious enthusiast of rare liberality, a profound philosopher, a poet, and author of great literary abilities and an intense lover of his species." Watters,

Coming to I-Tsing's time, we find that before joining the University, *Vyākaraṇa* or Grammar was the first thing that was taught. The name for general secular literature, as the traveller observes, was the *Vyākaraṇa* on which, at that time, there were five works, *viz.*, the *Siddha* composition for beginners, the Sūtra, the foundation of all grammatical science, the *Dhātu* consisting of one thousand slokas and treating particularly of grammatical roots, the fourth which was on the three *khilas*,[1] the fifth being the *Vṛtti-Sūtra*. Students learnt the book on the three *khilas* when they were ten years old, and had to study it for three years, which period was required for mastering it thoroughly. After all these, students had to study the *Vṛtti-Sūtra*, this being a commentary on Pāṇini's sūtra. Finishing them, they learnt composition in prose and verse. Next, attention had to be devoted to *Hetuvidyā* (Logic) and *Abhidarma-koṣa* (Metaphysics). In learning the *Nyāyadvāra-tarka-sāstra*, students had to draw *anumāna* (inferences). Then they studied the *Jātaka* (Buddhist birth-stories). That was the preliminary stage of study, after which a student could join the University. Here, as I-Tsing points out eminent and accomplished men assembled in crowds to discuss possible and impossible questions, and, after having been assured by wise men, of the excellence

Courses of Study

Yuan Chwang, II. 203. "Nāgārjuna may nave nourisnea any time between 125 and 200 A. D. A legend which makes him live for 300 years is not without significance, for he represents a movement and a school as much as a personality and if he taught in the second Century A. D., he cannot have been the founder of Mahāyānism. Yet he seems to be the first great name difinitely connected with it and the ascription to him of numerous later treatises, though unwarrantable, shows that his authority was sufficient to stamp a work or a doctrine as orthodox Mahāyānism". *Hinduism and Buddhism*, p. xxxii.

1 *Khila* means waste land, so called because this part of grammar may be likened to the way in which a farmer prepared his field for corn. It consisted of *Aṣṭadhātu* of one thousand slokas, *Maṇda* of the same number of slokas and *Unādi* which also consisted of the same number of slokas.

of their opinions became far-famed for their wisdom. After finishing their education in the University, the scholars proceeded to the king's court to present their schemes and show their talent, seeking for appointments[1].

While some scholars took to the services, others continued their studies when they had to read Patañjali's book, the *Bhartṛhari Sástra*, the *Vākya*—discourse, and the Vedas which they evidently studied to oppose the heretics[2]. It seems there was what we call now the tutorial method of teaching, for I-Tsing observes that he used to converse with his teachers so intimately that he was able to receive invaluable instruction personally from them[3]. And it is also clear that the University provided instruction not only for those who joined the order of monks, but for the laity also. And in concluding this portion of my lecture, I may add that just as we have the system of granting diplomas, in Nālandā the names of famous scholars were written in white on the lofty gates—a more permanent and conspicuous method of perpetuating the names of the scholars than what we have now-a-days.

Nālandā, as we know from Tibetan accounts, had a fine library, situated in the quarter known as the *Dharmagañja* (Piety Mart). It consisted of three grand buildings called *Ratṇasāgara*, *Ratṇadadhi* and *Ratṇarañjaka*, all associated with *Ratṇa*, *i. e.*, jewels, these being the three jewels of Buddhism,—Buddha, Dharma and Saṃgha. *Ratṇadadhi* was nine-storied, and in it were kept the sacred scripts, especially the *Prājnāpāramitā Sūtra.* We have already referred to the fact how the Library first fared at the hands of the Muslim invaders. The building was then repaired, but it was

1 *A Record of the Buddhist Religion*, p. 177.

2 *Ibid*, p. 181.

3 *Ibid*. p. 178.

finally destroyed by indigent Tirthaṇkaras who felt insulted and aggrieved at the treatment meted out to them, in consequence of which they brought about the destruction of the buildings by fire. Epigraphic evidence confirms the statement about the destruction of the building by fire and its re-building.[1]

Such was Nālandā. In bidding adieu to this subject we cannot but refer to one of its mottos which was :—

" *Conquer anger by pardon, conquer a bad man by good deeds, conquer a miser by giving him more, and conquer a liar by truth.*"

or

" *Dhamma and Adhamma both cannot give the same fruits : Adhamma drags one down to hell, while Dhamma leads one to Heaven.*"

Let us hope that in our University, also, the same truths will prevail.

---

1 *Vide*, ante p. 132.

LECTURE VI

The Royal University of Vikramasila

After having tried to give you some idea about the University of Nālandā, I now propose to deal with the Royal University of Vikramaśīlā. It is associated with the permanent epithet *Royal*, as it was not only created by a king, but it is also on record that the titles on scholars were bestowed by kings. And if the University of Nālandā fulfilled the dictum of Newman that a University is a school of universal learning, implying the assemblage of strangers from various places in one spot, this royal University of Vikramaśīlā, as we have already hinted in our fifth lecture, also satisfied the condition to a great extent. And it also satisfied the dictum of Carlyle of being a collection of books, for we know, both from internal and external evidence, that there was a big library, which, along with all its other paraphernalia, was destroyed at the time of the establishment of the Muhammadan power in Bihar.

Paucity of Accounts

The accounts, however, relating to Vikramśīlā are rather meagre. For the details, we have to depend to a large extent on Tāranāth, the historian of Tibet, whose name we have already mentioned several times. For translation of some passages relating to Vikramśīlā, I am indebted to Sister Gertrude of the local Convent, and I avail myself of this opportunity to render publicly my best thanks to her for helping me in elucidating the account of Vikramaśīlā.

Chinese Travellers

Our difficulty in tracing a fuller history of Vikramaśīlā is intensified by the fact that Hiuen Tsiang, the prince of Chinese travellers, has not given us any accounts of it proving that the University had not yet come into existence, or, at any rate, was not of sufficient importance to merit his visit, Neither does the other Chinese traveller, I-Tsing, to whom we are so much indebted regarding the curriculum of Nālandā, has thrown any light on it, showing that Nālandā, was still then *the* University of Northern India and that Vikramaśīlā was then unknown, and the presumption that it had been revived and forsaken, or at least had fallen into decay before, the coming of Hiuen Tsiang,[1] cannot at all hold good[2]. Vikramaśīlā began to rise after the downfall, at any rate, after the decadence of Nālandā, though for some time there was connection between the two. Lāmā Tāranāth remarks that the professors of Vikramaśīlā watched over the affairs of Nālandā.[3] It is very difficult to guess at the meaning of this, but, even in later times, there appears to have been some connection and we find that while Atiśa was proceeding towards Tibet, his Tibetan interpreter was staying at Nālandā.

The name of the University

While discussing the name of Nālandā, we referred to its derivation from a tradition, and here also we find a tradition telling us about the origin of the University, at any rate, of the monastery, which gave birth to the University. It is said to have been so named because a *Yakṣa* called Vikrama was suppressed here.[4] A Tibetan tradition also lays down that Āchāryya Kampilya, a learned professor of the school of Buddhist Tantras who had obtained the *siddhi* or perfection in the *Mahāmudrā* mysticism, was once struck with the features of a

---

1 *J. B. T. S.*, I.

2 "The inscriptions on the minor figures in Gupta character of the third and fourth centuries show that the *Vihār* with its chief cave had been established a considerable period before that time, probably at the beginning of the Christian era, or even earlier." *Ibid.* This is altogether a fanciful theory. The fact that it was founded by Dharmapāla who reigned in the ninth century, clearly demolishes the above

3 *Indian Pandits in the Land of Snow*, p. 66.

4 *J. B. T. S.*, Vol. I., 10—11.

bluff rocky hill which stood on the banks of the Ganges. Observing its peculiar fitness for the site of a *Vihār* he thought that, under royal auspices, it could be converted into a great place for the use of the *Saṃgha.* By dint of foreknowledge he also knew that at one time on that hill a great *Vihār* would be built. In course of time, Kampilya himself was born as Dharmapāla[1], the famous Buddhist king whom we have referred to in our first lecture, and remembering what he had been in his previous birth, he built the monastery and along with it the University. In view of the fact of the first donor being a king, Vikramaśīlā was known as the Royal University.

After all, this may be a story—one may call it a tradition—but we cannot altogether ignore tradition. And whatever may be the value of the above tradition, it is an admitted fact that the foundation of the monastery was first laid by Dharmapāla in the 9th century, *Paramasaugata Parameśvara Paramabhaṭṭāraka Mahārājādhirāja* Dharmapāla, the Buddhist King, who has already received some attention in our first lecture and who is mentioned in the Khālimpur *Praśasti*, the date of which has been fixed at 810 A. D. Here, under his royal auspices one hundred and eight professors taught various subjects[2]. In addition to these one hundred and eight teachers, there were also *Āchāryyas* for offering wood and fire, and for ordination, as well as three superintendents. That was the beginning of this great University. For four centuries it worked successfully, being managed, under royal patronage, by a board of six members presided over by the High Priest. It granted the diploma of Paṇḍita to all distinguished *alumni*,[3] the

Beginning of the University

1 *J. B. T. S.* Pt. I., p. 11.

2 *Ibid.* Vide, Schiefner, Tāranāth, p. 220

3 S. C. Vidyābhūṣana's *Indian Logic, Mediæval School*, p. 79. It is not known what title the University of Nālandā conferred on its

diploma being conferred by the reigning king. Among these Paṇḍitas can well be mentioned Ratṇa Vajra, an inhabitant of Kashmir, who received the royal diploma of the University and who was appointed a gate-keeper—a post of high distinction here also, as at Nālandā. Similarly there was Āchāryya Jetāri, who received from king Mahipāla the same diploma and who could boast of the great Dvīpaṇkara[1] as his pupil. Of the others, Ratṇa Kīrti, a professor at the University, deserved well to be mentioned along with Jñāna Srī Mitra, who was considered a pillar of the Vikramaśilā University. Atiśa or Dvīpaṇkara himself was indebted to him. Jñāna-Srī Mitra was also a gate-keeper and was appointed head of the University when Atiśa left for Tibet. We may also mention the name of Ratṇākara Sānti, who was ordained in the order of the Sarvāstivāda school of Odandapura, of which we shall speak later on, and who learnt the Sūtra at Vikramaśīlā from Jetāri,[2] Ratṇākara Kīrti and others. He is said to have flourished during the reign of Mahipāla and is reputed to be the author of one hundred books, including Taṇtras and Sutras. Ratṇākara was also made a gate-keeper, after which at the invitation of the king of Ceylon he visited that island where he gave an impetus to the Buddhist doctrine[3].

The Gates of the University

We thus note here some difference between Nālandā and Vikramaśīlā Universities, for in the former we see only one *Dvārapaṇḍita*, or gate-keeper, who tested the

---

distinguished students. M. M. S. C. Vidyābhūṣana suggested that that University also recognised the title of Paṇdits.

1 According to Babu Harendra Nath Ghosh B. A,, Dvīpaṇkara was trained in the Vihār of Vajāsana near Sābhāra in Vikramapura, vide *Dacca Review*, 1921.

2 For an account of Jetāri, see Schiefner's *Tāranāth*, p. 230; also, Vidyābhūsana's *Logic*, 136. Jetāri hailed from Varendra (Northern Bengal).

3 S. C. Vidyābhūṣana's, *Indian Logic, Medæival School*, p. 342. Ratnākara bore the title of Mahāpaṇdita,

merits of students anxious to enter the University, but here were six gates guarded by six Paṇḍitas. It may be, that each of these six colleges, specialising in a particular subject, with the gate-keeper as its Principal, taught a particular branch of knowledge, thus guarding collectively the destinies of Vikramaśilā.[1] According to Tāranāth, there were Prajñākaramati at the southern gate, Ratṇākara Śānti guarded the eastern gate, Vāgīsvara Kīrti watched over the destinies of the western gate, Naropanta ruled at the northern gate, Ratṇa Vajra was in charge of the first central gate and Jñāna Śrī Mitra tested students at the second central gate.[2]

The Vikramaśilā standard was higher than the one at Nālandā regarding academic organisation, but it could neither attain the wide range of influence of Nālandā, nor had it the vast numerical strength of the latter, though it too, had a large student population. The character of the times, of course, was more or less responsible for it. The whole country was suffering from a disruption, and Magadha which was gradually declining and losing fast its independent existence by coming under Bengal, was more or less playing a second fiddle. Nevertheless, the University was a large establishment. Dharmapāla, its founder, furnished it with four establishments, each consisting of 27 monks belonging to the four principal sects. He also endowed it with rich grants, fixing regular allowances for the maintenance of priests and students. Besides the above, there were establishments for temporary residents.[3] As was the case with the Nālandā University, the kings after Dharmapāla made other additions to the Univer-

The Establishment

1 According to Tāranāth, Prajñākaramati flourished during the reign of King Chanaka. (p. 135).

2 *Tāranāth*, 235.

3 *J. B. T. S.*, 1—10.

sity. There was a central hall, called the House of Science. It had six gates which opened on its six colleges, each having one hundred and eight professors. There was also a large open space which could hold an assembly of 8,000 persons.[1]

Each college was under the guidance of a *Dvāra Paṇḍita*, (the Paṇḍita at the gate) referred to above. Just as at Nālandā, students desirous of entering the University had to subject themselves to a severe test examination, here also no one could enter the precincts of this seat of learning without defeating the *Dvāra Paṇḍita* in controversial disquisition. At any rate, following the example of Nālandā, every student desirous of higher teaching had to submit to an examination, though there is nothing on record as to the percentage of failure, as we have, thanks to Hiuen Tsiang, at Nālandā. The two Paṇḍitas who taught theology in the central college were called the first and second "pillars" of the University. For the support of the resident pupils of the colleges within the monastery, there were *Satras* (free board hostels), where scholars were entertained free and supplied with necessaries. They were endowed, as at Nālandā, by the princes and nobles of the country. That this sort of endowment very likely continued from the beginning till the end of the University, is proved by the fact that as late as the tenth century, a *Satra* was added to the Vihāra by one of the sons of King Sanātana of Varendra, better known by his name of Jetāri. Like Nālandā, the University was surrounded by a wall. In its front wall, on the right of the principal entrance, was painted the likeness of Nāgārjuna, once the head of the Nālandā University, and on the left the portrait of Atiśa himself, who figured

1 "The quardrangle evidently was a large Buddhist monastery or Vihāra, such as at one time existed at Sārnath, Sānchi, Budh-gayā and other places of note". Dr. R. L. Mitra.

prominently at Vikramaśilā. We also find the existence of a *Dharmaśālā* at the gate outside the wall, where strangers arriving late after the closing of the gate were sheltered. The whole thing must have been a magnificent one and it was evidently so finely adapted to the purpose for which it was constructed, considering it both as a religious and an educational institution, that the Tibetans took it as a model for one of their monasteries.

Courses of study

The courses of study at Vikramaśīlā were perhaps less comprehensive than those at Nālandā. But here, as at Nālandā, teaching was both tutorial and professorial. Buddhistic teaching aimed very much at what we call the tutorial system. Every novice was required to choose a *Bhikṣu*, who was a full member of the order, as his preceptor or *Āchāryya*, and cordial and intimate relationship was expected between the teacher and the taught. The *Mahāvagga* prescribed that the *Āchāryya* was to consider the pupil as a son, while the pupil was to look upon the teacher as father, so that the two united by mutual reverence, confidence and communion of life, might progress and reach a high stage in doctrine and discipline. The student was to receive all assistance from his *Āchāryya* not only in the matter of spiritual help but also in teaching, while the teacher was to put questions to him and to improve his condition by exhortation and instruction, just as is done in the present day tutorial classes.

Study of Tāntrikism

Perhaps the most important branch of learning taught here was the Tantras. Vikramaśīlā flourished in the days of Tāntrikism, when occult sciences and magic had become favourite subjects of study. It was really from the fifth century that Buddhism assumed a new phase and changed its nature into that of Tāntrikism which developed further between the eighth and tenth centuries of the Christian era. As Dr. Kern, the great authority on Buddhism, has rightly observed,[1] "The doctrine of Buddhism in India from the eighth century downwards nearly coincides with the growing influence of Tāntrikism and sorcery which stand to each other in the relation of theory to practice". The development of Tāntrikism is a feature that Buddhism and Hinduism have in common. Having once commenced the work of importation and assimilation, it went on and became ere long a new thing. "The development of the infatuating Tāntrikism, which practically verges on sorcery claiming a religious basis, attracted the notice of the Mahāyāna school and ere long the idolatrous cult of "female energies" was founded, grafted upon the theistic Mahāyāna and the pantheistic mysticism of Yoga"[2]. There was in the monastery of Vikramaśīlā a class of Tāntrikas, called by the name of *Kiṃsukha*, who brought on much trouble to Atiśa, the head of the University. The two instances referred to in *The Journal of the Buddhist Text Society*,[3] the one of Maitri, belonging to the *Kiṃsuka* class, who was charged with certain irregularities connected with doctrinal, ritual and other collateral matters, on account of which some thing condemnatory was written on the wall at the entrance of the Vihāra by a monk called Śānti, and the other, when a quantity of wine was detected in the possession of the same monk which he kept secretly in his room and which he was alleged to have brought for presenting to a Buddhist nun whom he intended to consult on certain matters, show how the religion of Gautama Buddha had deteriorated in the hands of his later followers.

Other courses of study

Next to the Tantras, there were studied Grammar, Metaphysics, and Logic. The last subject, which was studied assiduously and extensively at the Nālandā

1 Kern's *Buddhism*, p. 133.

N. N. Vasu, *Modern Buddhism.*

Part of a frieze at Vikramasila.
(Known as the Ananta Sayya)

Another part of the frieze.
(Known as the marriage of Rama & Sita)

To face p. 153.

University was also cultivated here, and some of the greatest scholars at Vikramaśīlā distinguished themselves in this subject. The fact that the *Dvāra Paṇḍitas*, or gate-keepers, were eminent logicians goes to prove that Logic was evidently a popular subject[1].

And here also, as at Nālandā, the teachers and students occupied themselves with copying manuscripts, and in the British Museum there is a beautiful copy of the *Aṣṭa Sāhasrika Prajñāpāramitā*, the colophon of which mentions the fact of its being copied in the reign of *Parameśvara Paramabhattāraka Paramasaugata Mahārādhirāja Srimad* Gopāla Deva, who according to Dr. Barnett, was the second Gopāla Deva.[2]

Rai Bahadur S. C. Das, in his interesting work *Indian Pandits in the Land of Snow*, a book which is becoming rare, though published only thirty years back, has given us a graphic description of a religious assembly at Vikramaśīlā—corresponding to the Convocation of our days. The description is by the Tibetan who was sent there to take Atiśa for the renaissance of Buddhism in Tibet. "In the morning at 8 o'clock when the monks congregated together being conducted by the *Sthavira*, I was given a seat in the rank of the learners. Then first of all the venerable Vidyā Kokila came to preside over the assembly. His appearance was noble and majestic. He got exalted and steady like the *Sumeru* mountain. I asked those near me, if he was not Lord Atiśa". "What do you say, O Tibetan *Ayusmat*! This is the very revered Lāmā Vidyā Kokila who, being a lineal disciple of Āchāryya Chandra Kīrti, has become a saintly sage. Do you not know that he was the teacher of Atiśa?" Then, again pointing to another Āchāryya who was seated at the head of a row, I enquired if he was not Atiśa. I was told that he

A Convocation

1 *Indian Logic, Mediæval School*, p. 150.

2 *J. R. A. S.*, 1910, p. 151.

was the venerable Naropanta, who, for his scholarship in the sacred literature, had no equal among the Buddhists. He too was Atiśa's tutor. At this time when my eyes were moving to find out Atiśa, the Rājā of Vikramaśīlā came and took an exalted seat, but none of the monks, old or young, rose from their seats to mark his arrival.[1]

"Another Pandit came in a grave and solemn mood moving slowly. Many young *Ayusmats* rose from their seats to receive him with offerings of incense. The Rājā also rose from his seats to do him honour. On the Rājā's rising up, the monks and the Pandits also got up from their seats, respectively. The Lama was seated on a reserved seat. Thinking that, as so much honour was shown to the Lama, he must be some royal monk or some venerable *Sthavira* or Atiśa himself, I wished to know who he was. I was told that he was Vīravajra, a stranger whose residence was not known to them. When I interrogated how learned he was, they said that they were not aware of the extent of his attainments.

"When all the rows of seats were filled up there came Lord Atiśa, the venerable of venerables, in all his glory, at whose sight the eyes felt no satiety. His graceful appearance and smiling face struck every one of the assembly. From his waist hung down a bundle of keys. The Indians, Nepalese and Tibetans, all looked at him and took him for a countryman of their own. There was brightness mixed with simplicity of expression on his face which acted as a magic spell upon those who beheld him."

Such was Atiśa.[2] He was born in the royal family

1 This seems to be rather inexplicable. For later on, we find that on the Rājā's getting up, all the monks and the Paṇḍitas also got up. Of course, the ideal in ancient India indicated that the position of a student not to speak of a teacher, was higher than that of a king.

2 "Atisa revived the practice of the pure Mahāyāna doctrine by

of Gauḍ. In his early age he was known as Chandragarva and he was sent to Jetāri for his education. Under this great teacher, he studied the five kinds of sciences and thereby paved his way for the study of philosophy and religion. As he grew in age, he acquired proficiency in the three *Piṭakas* of the Mahāyāna doctrine, the high metaphysics of the Madhyamika and Yogīchāryyā schools and the four classes of Tantras. He then abandoned the world, commenced the study of the meditative science of the Buddhists and for this purpose came to a Vihāra, where the name of Guhyajñanā Vajra was given to him and he was initiated into the mysteries of esoteric Buddhism. At the age of nineteen he took the sacred vow from S'ila Rakṣita, the Mahāsaṇgika Āchāryya of the Odandapura University, who gave him the name of Dvīpaṇkara S'rījñāna. He then went to Suvarṇadvīpa, then the headquarters of Buddhism in East, and after residing there for twelve years returned to Magadha where he was acknowledged as the chief. He maintained the superiority of Magadha in religious discussions and in the reign of Naya Pāla accepted the post of High Priest at Vikramaśilā. He was taken to Tibet, after two unsuccessful missions, [1] by the envoy of the Tibetan king to bring about the renaissance

Atisa

---

showing the right way to the ignorant and misguided Lāmās of Tibet of its foreign and heretic elements which had completely tarnished it and restored it to its former purity and splendour." S. C. Das, Life of Atiśa in *J. A. S. B.*, IX. 1891, 46—53. "The influence of Atiśa was undoubtedly exercised in the direction of an everlarging diffusion of these images (illustrating the life of the Buddha) from any Tāntric calamities. The opulent lives of Queen Māyā (the scene of the nativity), the somewhat languid grace of the young Bodhisattva (the life of pleasure in the women's apartments) show in the details of the dress and of the bodies, the influences of Magadha which were introduced by Atiśa." *The Influence of Indian Art*, 136.

1 We know very little of the introduction of Buddhism into Tibet. In A. D. 632, the first Buddhist King of Tibet sent an envoy to India to secure the Buddhist scriptures. Hiuen Tsiang says that in his time Tibet was Buddhistic, but I-Tsing, who came later, says that Tibet had no Buddhism. See *ante* p. 129.

of Buddhism in that country. It was this Atiśa who was selected and who revived the practice of the Mahāyāna doctrine. He cleared the Buddhism of Tibet of foreign and heretic elements that had vitiated it and restored it to its former purity and splendour. Under his guidance, the misguided and ignorant Lāmās of Tibet discovered what is called the "real and pure path of the exalted excellence."[1] After a residence of thirteen years which was distributed over the different provinces of Tibet, during which he assiduously devoted himself to the propagation of pure Buddhism, enjoying uninterruptedly the good will and veneration of the people, Atiśa died there at the advanced age of seventy-three. He is still remembered with deep veneration all over Tibet.

It is interesting to note that neither Atiśa, nor his activities in Tibet, are mythical. Modern-day research proves this fact. *The Archæological Survey Report*[2] says the following :—

"The times of Atiśa have become known through Das's *Indian Pandits in the Land of Snow.* But up to the present it has been found impossible to decide whether the persons mentioned in connection with Atiśa actually lived or not. In the course of our tour we discovered several inscriptions of these times at Poo, in Spiti and Ladakh.

"On one of the walls of Tabo monastery of Spiti, I discovered an inscription of the days of King Byangchub-od of Guge, the very ruler who had invited Atiśa to Tibet. The principal hall of the Tabo monastery called Nam-par-snang-mdzad, seems to have remained unchanged since the days of Atiśa."[3] The writer also mentions

1 *Indian Pandits in the Land of Snow*, p. 76.

2 *Historical Documents from the Borders of Tibet, A. S. R.*, 1909-10.

3 Mr. E. H. Walsh, in his Foreword to *The Rambles in Bihar*, observes : "With reference to Atiśa, the Buddhist hierarch of Magadha

an inscription which contains the names of the two most important Lāmās of the periods, *viz.*, Rin-chen bsng-po and Atiśa, the latter being known as Phul-byung, his Tibetan name. The inscription says that Rin-chen was made a "light of wisdom" through the agency of Atiśa. This apparently is a reference to the controversy between the two Lāmās which ended with Rin-chen's acknowledging Atiśa's superiority."

Such was the head of the Vikramaśilā University which had a number of *alumni*. But such are the ravages of time that not only its glories have totally vanished, but it is even difficult to identify the site now. Cunningham suggested the village of Silāo near Borgāon. This is out of the question, as the Ganges could never have been near it.[1] Then there was the suggestion of the late lamented Mahāmahopādhyāya Dr. S. C. Vidyābhuṣaṇa, who tried to identify it with Sultānganj in Bhagalpur.[2] The hill here is a very small one, too small to have a monastery with six gates and a quadrangle or open space which could hold an assembly of 8000 men and also the large number of temples and colleges it contained. This identification also is, therefore, anything but satisfactory. The Tibetan chronicles, which are the best authorities on this subject, mention clearly that the monastery was situated on a bluff hill on the right bank of the river Ganges. The best identification is that by Mr. Nundo Lal De who observes[3]:—" A day's sail below Sultanganj is situated a projecting steep hill called

Identification of Site

who ruled over the Vikramasila monastery in the eleventh century and who at the invitation of the king of Tibet, visited that country and reformed the form of the Buddhistic religion then prevailing there, it is interesting to note that his tomb still exists at Nyethang in Tibet, and the paintings on it and on the walls of the chapel which adjoins it, are the most artistic that I saw while in Tibet."

1 *A. S. R.*, VIII, 75.

2 *J. A. S. B.*, 1909.

3 *J. A. S. B.*, Vol. V., No. 1, p. 7.

Pātharghāta which is a spur of the Colgong range. It is about six miles to the north of Colgong, twenty-four miles to the east of Bhagalpur, and twenty-eight miles to the east of Champānagar, the ancient Champā, the capital of Aṅga. The rocky projections at Pātharghāṭā and Colgong form a beautiful curve on the right bank of the Ganges, flanked by an amphitheatre of hills, which greatly enhances the picturesqueness of the landscape and heightens its beauty. The river Ganges, the general course of which from Bhagalpur to the ocean is nearly due east, flows northward from Colgong to Pātharghāṭā and takes a singular turn round the Pātharghāṭā hill, some of the rocks of which project in a promontory into the river, and this projecting portion with a large part of the hill behind, is properly called Pātharghāṭā."[4]

The site suggested by Mr. De is very likely the site of the Vikramaśīlā monastery which was situated on a bluff hill, as the Tibetan chronicles say, on the right bank of the Ganges and it has a sufficient space for a congregation of 8000, with many temples and buildings. The monastery was destroyed by the followers of Islam when they invaded Magadha—a point which we will take up presently, after referring to another University, namely that of Odandapura, which also shared the same fate as that of Vikramaśīlā.

Rai Bahadur Sarat Chandra Das expressed the opinion [1] 'that on account of the foundation of a city in the neighbourdood of Nālandā, which became the capital of Magadha under the Pāla kings, and on account of the great eminence to which the monastery itself arose, the entire province came to be known by the name of Vihār and the older name of Magadha gradually

4 We regret the premature death of Mr. De who has done so much for ancient Indian cultnre, by his valuable contribution, notably, the *Ancient Geography of India*.

1 *Hindustan Review*, 1906, p. 190.

came to be forgotten. This seems to be a mere guess for which the late Rai Bahadur did not cite any authority, nor does the late Dr. V. A. Smith cite any other than that or Tāranāth for his statement that Gopāla, the first of the Pāla dynasty[1], "founded a great monastery at Uddandapura or Odantapuri," as it is sometimes called, this being at any rate the ancient name of the modern town of Bihār. This name has also been used by Tāranāth. The Muhammdan historian, Abu Umar Minhajuddin Usman i. n Sirajuddin at Juzanni, better known as Minhaj, whom we have to depend upon for facts relating to the history of Northen India of this period, mentioned the place as Adwand Bihar.

Epigraphic references

References to epigraphic evidence about Odandapura are not many. We have, however, one in the inscription inscribed in the second regnal year of king Surapāla Deva of the Pāla dynasty in which we note the flourishing condition of the Vihār. And we have another similar inscription referring to the same thing, both being, unfortunately, now at Calcutta. Both are inscribed on two standing Buddha figures, in one the Buddha is subjugating an infuriated elephant, while in the other he is being worshipped by Indra and Brahmā.[2]

There is another epigraphic evidence, inscribed in the ninth regnal year of Nārāyaṇāpāla Deva, in which one Dharmamitra, an inhabitant of the Andhra country, established an image of Buddha. Mr. R. D. Banerjee[3]

---

1 *The Early History of India*, p. 413. Tāranāth says; "Gopāla, ruling in the beginning of his life in Bengal, founded in the neighbourhood of Odantapura the Vihāra ot Nālandā and after he had instituted in both countries many schools of the clergy, he made a great sacrifice to the Law" (p. 158). This would imply that Nālandā came after Odandapura, which is not a fact. Tāranāth in another place (p. 193), however, observes: "At the time of king Gopāla and Devapāla, Odantapura Vihāra was erected."

2 *Bangiya Sāhitya Parisat Patrikā*, Vol. XV, p. 12.

3 *History of Bengal*, Vol. I, p. 198. *Vide* also *Bangiya Sāhitya Parisat Patrikā*, Vol. XV, p. 13.

is of opinion that very likely the place where this image was installed was Odandapura. The image is not in existence, but the portion containing the inscription is at Calcutta.

In the fifty-fourth regnal year of the same king, Nārāyaṇapala Deva, the figure of the goddess Pārvatī was installed at Odandapura. The name Odandapura is also mentioned in the inscription.[1]

As late as in 1891 was taken to the Calcutta Museum a figure of the goddess Tārā discovered also at Odandapura. In this there is an inscription of the second regnal year of Rāmapāla, about whom and his life *Rāmacharita*, discovered by Mahāmahopādhyaya H.:P. Sastri, we have spoken in our first lecture.

And if I may be permitted to go further, for this does not really come within the period we are describing, I may mention that an inscription in Arabic was discovered at the same place incised in 1242.[2]

Odandapura was destroyed in 1199 when Muhammad, the son of Bakhtiar, invaded Magadha. If we are to rely on Tāranāth, it would appear that before the final destruction, there was another attempt. Tāranāth gives a fanciful story that a minister of the Turuska king, out of the Karṇa land in the west, together with 500 Turks came to Magadha to plunder. They plundered the sacrificial materials, but when they began to walk all in a body to the *Āchāryya* Kamala Raksita, he got into a rage and walked up along, throwing a jug filled with water, over which he had spoken *mantras*. The result was that the Turks all fled and many were killed. Making every allowance, we must say, that the historian refers to the failure of the first attack. Laksmana Sena was then the king of Bengal. According to the Muhammadan historian, Minhaz, whom we have referred

1 *Indian Antiquary*, 1918, p. 110.

2 *J. A. S. B.*. Old Series, XII—12,45.

to before and whom we will have to quote again, Magadha was attacked after the eightieth regnal year of Laksmana Sen. As the Laksmana era had its commencement in 1119, the date of the conquest falls in 1199. That was the year of the destruction of all the Buddhistic places of learning in Bihar, Nālandā, Vikramaśīla and Odandapura. Nuddea was attacked in the following year.[1]

Destruction by the Muhammadans

That Muhammad captured these seats of learning and destroyed them in that year, is further borne out by the fact that the colophon of *Pañchakara* in the library of the University of Cambridge contains the fact that Odandapura was destroyed in the thirty-eighth regnal year of Govindapāladeva about whom we spoke in some detail in our first lecture. As Govindapāladeva's accession dates from 1161, the date of the destruction of these monasteries comes to 1199.

Description by a Muhammadan historian

I have already hinted that Muhammad Bakhtiyar's attacks on Magadha, before he ventured on those holy places which he rightly considered to be seats of wealth also, were in the nature of incursions. As Minhaz has observed, "Being a bold and enterprising man, he used to make incursions into the districts of Munair[2] and Bihar and bring away much plunder, until in this manner he obtained plenty of horses, arms and men. The fame of his bravery and of his plundering raids spread abroad and a body of Khiljis joined him from Hindustan. His exploits were reported to Sultan Kutbuddin and he sent him a dress and showed him great honour. Being thus encouraged, he led his army into Bihar and ravaged it.

1 Tāranāth, p. 94, says that the Turks, conquered the whole of Magadha and destroyed many Vihāras, "In Śrī Nālandā much damage was done and the priests fled abroad." On p. 262, he further observes, that when Magadha was conquered the scholars went out and spread the doctrine everywhere.

2 Elliot identified Munair as Monghyr. This was a mistake. Munair is the modern Munair in the district of Patna. Vide *Journal of the Bihar and Orissa Research Society*, vol. I.

In this manner, he continued for a year or two to plunder the neighbourhood and at last prepared to invade the country. He went to the gate of the fort of Bihar with only two hundred horse and began the war by taking the enemy unawares."

Minhaz goes on: "Muhammad-i-Bakhtyar, threw himself into the postern of the gate-way of the place and gained possession of the place. Great plunder fell into the hands of the victims. Most of the inhabitants of the place were Brahmans with shaven heads. They were all slain. There were a great number of books which came under the observation of the Musalmans. They summoned a number of Hindus that they might give them information respecting the import of these books, but all the Hindus had been killed. On becoming acquainted, it was found that the whole of the fortress and city was a college and in the Hindi tongue, they called a college Bihar". Tāranāth also supports this account. He observes, "In the country between the Ganges and the Jumna the Turuṣka king appeared and by means of several Bhikṣus who were his messengers, he with other small kings of the Turuṣkas living in Bengal and other parts of the country, invaded. and he conquered the whole of Magadha, killed many clerics in Odandapura, destroyed this as well as Vikramaśīla, and on the spot of the old Vihāra a fortress of the Turuṣkas was erected."[1]

Blow to Indian Buddhism

The University of Vikramaśila, which also must have attracted the bold Muslim adventurer, shared the same fate. Indian Buddhism received a great blow, at any rate received a blow from the effect of which it has not been able to recover. A large party of the Buddhist population was forced to leave the country, while others embraced the faith of Islam. As Dr. Waddel has ob-

---

1 Tāranāth, Text, p. 56. Tāranāth has it also that the king of Magadha had erected fortresses both at Odandapura and Vikramaśilā where he had placed some soldiers.

served,[1] "In the declining days of Indian Buddhism, when its spiritual and regenerating influences were almost dead, the Muhammadan invasion swept over India, in the latter end of the twelfth century A. D., and effectually stamped Buddhism out of the country. The Afghan soldiery especially attacked the Buddhistic monasteries, with their teeming idols and they massacred the monks wholesale; and as the Buddhist religion, unlike the more domestic Brahmanism, is dependent on its priests and monks for its vitality, it soon disappeared in the absence of the latter." As Minhaz says, "It is said by credible persons that he went to the gate of the fort of Bihar with only two hundred horse, and began the war by taking the enemy unwares. When Bakhtiyar reached the gate of the fort, and the fighting began, Muhammad Bakhtiyar with great vigour and audacity rushed in at the gate of the fort and gained possession of the place. Great plunder fell into the hands of the victors. Most of the inhabitants of the place were Brahmans with shaven hands. They were put to death. Large numbers of books were found here, and when the Muhammadans saw them, they called for some persons to explain their contents, but all the men had been killed. It was discovered that the whole fort and city was a place of study. In the Hindi language the word Behar (Vihār) means a College.[2]

Much is attempted to be made out regarding this destruction of the monks and their monasteries. But two things have to be considered in this connection. We learn from Tāranāth, that both in Odandapura as well as in Vikramaśīlā, the Magadhan king made a kind of fortress where some warriors had been installed. It is also on record that the monks had joined with the guards in repulsing the invaders. Further, as Sir P. C. Roy,

1 Waddel's *Lamaism*, p. 16.
2 Tabakat-i-Nasiri, p. 306.

relying on manuscripts, has observed, "The monasteries had degenerated into hotbeds of corruption, so much so that the Mussalman conquerors felt little compunction in putting the inmates thereof to the sword."[1]

Again, the spirit of the times justified such massacres. Let us look at the capture of Baghdad by the Mughals, who were then Buddhists, under Halaku. Mutasim repaired to the Mongal camp when the savage chief concealed the perfidy of his designs under the mask of smooth words and a friendly reception. Halaku then requested the Caliph to send word into the city that the armed inhabitants should throw away their weapons, and assemble before the gates, in order that a general census might be taken. Under the orders of the Caliph, the city poured out its unarmed defenders who were immediately secured. The next day, at sunrise, Halaku issued commands for the sack of the devoted city and the massacre of its inhabitants. The women and the children were trampled to death. Delicately nurtured ladies, who had never braved the sight of crowds, were dragged into the open streets and subjected to the grossest brutalities; the artistic and literary treasures collected with such labour and industry by sovereign after sovereign, together with the remains of the old Persian civilisation, were destroyed in the course of a few hours. For three days the streets ran with blood, and the water of the Tigris was dyed red for miles along its course. The horrors of rapine, slaughter and outraged humanity lasted for six weeks. The palaces, mosques, and mausolea were destroyed by fire or levelled to the earth for their golden domes. The patients in the hospitals, and the students and professors in the colleges, were put to the sword. In the academies the immortal works of great and learned men were reduced

1 *A History of Hindu Chemistry*, XXXIX.

to ashes; books were thrown into the fire, or, when the Tigris was near, buried in its waters. The accumulated treasures of five centuries were thus for ever lost to humanity and the flower of the nation was completely destroyed. After the carnage had lasted for four days, Mutasim was beaten to death together with his sons and the principal members of his family.[1]

As Mr. Arnold has aptly expressed it: "There is no event in the history of Islam that for terror and destruction can be compared to the Mongal conquest. Like an avalanche, the hosts of Chingiz Khan swept over the centres of Muslim culture and civilisation, leaving behind them bare deserts and shapeless ruins where before had stood stately cities girt about with gardens and fruitful corn land". Well might the Muhammadan historian shudder to relate such horrors! "For many years I shrank from giving a recital of these events on account of their magnitude and my abhorrence. Even now I come reluctant to the task, for who would deem it a light thing to sing the death song of Islam and of the Muslim, or find it easy to tell this tale? Oh that my mother had not given me birth! Oh, would that I had died ere this, and been a thing forgotten, forgotten quite."[2] Just as Bahgdad, the abode of learning, the seat of culture, the eye and centre of the saracenic world, was ruined for ever, so were Vikramaśila and Odandapura, the seats and centres of Buddhistic world and culture, destroyed for ever, and with their downfall was sounded the death-knell of Buddhism in India and for some centuries the gloom of night fell on Eastern India. The invasion of the Muslims, so far as the Buddhistic monasteries were concerned, was a great calamity, but history merely repeated itself here. With the fall of the Buddhist Universities, Buddhism disappeared from this part of the

1 Ameer Ali, *A short History of the Saracens*, pp. 397 and 398.

2 Arnold, *The Preaching of Islam*, p. 218.

country and with it Buddhistic learning. The Hindu Universities of Nuddea and Mithi lāwhich came later on, were purely Brāhmaṇic ones. As Dr. Kern, one of the best authorities on Buddhism, observes, "In consequence of the invasion of the country by the Muhammadans, the monasteries of Vikramaśilā and Odandapura were destroyed and the monks were killed, or fled to other countries. The learned Sākya S'rī went to Orissa and afterwards to Tibet. Many emigrants from Magadha rejoined their brethren in the south and founded colleges on a modest scale. Buddhism lingered in the remotest parts of the peninsula to which the invaders could not readily penetrate."

Muhammadan Invasion and Buddhism

It has been suggested by learned authorities like Kern and Waddell, that Buddhism in India received its death-blow because of the Muhammadan attack. But that was not the only cause, there were other causes as great as this. Indian Buddhism at that time was not the Buddhism of Asoka; it was Tāntrikism, worshipping of female energy in conjunction with male energy. It had degenerated from its great philosophical and speculative height more or less to demonology, while there was very little spiritual and regenerating influence left in it. It was a curious admixture of alchemical processes on the one hand, and grotesque and obscure and sometimes revolting rites, on the other. There was more of materialism in it, than the purely spiritual ideals of Gautama Buddha. Even in the time of Nāgārjuna, who, both by example and theory, taught that Brahmā, Viṣṇu, Siva, Tārā and other deities possessed the attributes which the Brāhmaṇas had assigned to them and therefore were the proper objects of worship for help, it was gradually leaning towards Hinduism which was re-establishing itself. The causes which brought about the downfall of Buddhism were working from within. The purity of life and the austerity of practices enjoined on the followers of the creed, became in the long run irksome. They found it extremely difficult to continue them. And, again, the monasteries were degenerating into hotbeds of corruption. Hinduism, also, was swallowing up Buddhism and acknowledging the founder of this religion as an Avatāra, or incarnation, of *Viṣṇu.* Buddhism had made so many compromises that in the end it became iudistinguishable from Hinduism. Even from the seventh century itself, the development of the infatuating Tāntrikism, which reached its climax by the eleventh century and which practically verged on sorcery claiming a religious basis, attracted the notice of the Mahāyāna school, and ere long the idolatrous cult of female energies was found grafted upon Mahāyāna and the pantheistic mysticism of Yoga. And this Tāntrika phase of the Mahāyāna school reached its climax when it adapted and assimilated to itself the theory of the Kālachakra. It went even far[1]. A mysterious union was established between the goddess Kāli and the Buddhas. The doctrine of Buddha went on further in its depraved course—importation, assimilation and compromise—and all these had their due as well as undue share and the way was paved for its disappearance. The cause which favoured the rise and progress of the Hindu Tantras equally contributed to the development of the Buddhistic ones, only in the latter case, instead of S'iva or Pārvatī, a Buddha, a Tathāgata, or an Avalokiteśvara is often addressed in the invocation as the source and fountain of all knowledge. We have also a class of Tantras which are an admixture of Buddhistic and Śaiva cult.[2]

The Pāla kings were Buddhists, and they tried to give a new turn to their faith. They encouraged Buddhist religion by patronage, and by the starting of

1 N. N. Vasu, *Modern Buddhism*, p. 4.

2 Sir P. C. Roy, *A History of Hindu Chemistry*, XV.

Buddhistic Universities. A large number of learned men, like Atiśa, flourished under their patronage. These scholars, though professedly belonging to the Tāntrika cult, rose above it, but they could not prevent the downward course. The goal of life adopted by the majority of the Buddhists was emancipation, but to them it became attainable only through enjoyment, life being indissolubly linked with weal and woe. Love and enjoyment of the world predominated. In addition to this, I venture to submit that there was another cause.

The Pāla Kings and Buddhism

The Pāla kings were Buddhists, but they were not at all aggressive Buddhists, nor were they so powerful. Further, they were all too tolerant. The facts that Dharmapāla's *Mahāsammata* could establish a big Viṣṇumandira at a place called Subbasthali, and that a *liṅgam*[1] could be set up at Buddha Gaya, while a grant could be made by Madanapāla to a Brāhmaṇa as *dakṣiṇā* for reading the *Mahābhārata* to the queens—all these show that the Buddhism of the Pāla Kings could not have been of any aggressive character. Hinduism was re-establishing itself and making itself supreme over the so-called Buddhism. The kings were not powerful enough to bring about the permanent renaissance of Buddhism, while the very form of the extant religion of Siddhārtha, coupled with its want of spirituality,—the true life of any religion,—had already prepared the way for the downfall of Buddhism, and the Mussalman irruptions only made it come down like a house of sand which was already too much shattered. The temple at Buddha Gaya, which had been the centre of devotees, had again fallen into the hands of the *Snātakas*.[2] It had no wealth, while the monasteries were full of it. The Muhammadan invaders plundered and destroyed Odandapura and Vikramaśilā, but although Buddha Gaya was not even fifty

1 *Mahābodhi*, XXVIII, 3.

2 See *Gauḍa Lekhamālā*, p. 32.

miles from the former, Muhammad Ibn Bakhtiyar did not think it worth while to attack it. As Dr. Bloch has suggested, "so far as Muhammadan invaders were concerned, no serious damage appears to have occurred to the Bodhi tree. The object which led those wild sons of the Central Asian desert to the destruction and desecration of so many a famous temple in India was not religious zeal only. I am afraid we should be over-estimating them, if we did not admit that a certain delight in plunder might have helped to swell the army of Bakhtiyar Khilji when he made his first inroad into Bihar and Bengal towards the close of the twelfth century. But he did not proceed to Bodh-gaya, for the simple reason that a *pipul* tree certainly was no object worth "looting". Or, in other words, even the place of *bodhi* of Gautama had lost its importance."[1]

Indeed Buddha Gaya had lost its eminence ; it was not the centre of attractiom for Buddhist pilgrims. Hinduism was re-asserting itself. The Muhammadan invasion helped it at the cost of Buddhism. Even when Fa-hien was here, although he saw everything as a Buddhist devotee, we find that Hinduism of the orthodox kind was prominent and even sacrifices were permitted. Mr. V. A. Smith was perfectly right when he observed that, "the Brahmanical reaction against Buddhism had begun at a time considerably earlier than that of Fa-hien's travels, and Indian Buddhism was already upon the downward path."[2] We may go even further back. The reaction against the religion of the Buddha had become apparent even at the time of Puṣyamitra's celebration of the horse-sacrifice in the second century B. C. Samudragupta and, after him, his grandsons followed. The recrudescence of Brahmanical Hinduism was clear during the Gupta period. The Muhammadan

1 *Archæological Survey Report*, 1908—09.

2 *The Early History of India*, *p*.

invasion helped to bring it down in Bihar. That was the last vestige of Buddhism in these parts, though it lingered for a while in the minds of some sections of the people. The surviving ministers migrated to Orissa, founded colleges in southern India[1] and stopped the tide of extinction by building *chaityas* and stūpas. That question, however, is beyond the scope of our subject.

It is a curious fact that all the three Universities,—Nālandā, Odandapura and Vikramaśīlā,—were situated at some distance from the Capital or capitals of Magadha. What was the reason for it? I venture to think that the best answer to such a question has been given by the great Rabindranath in his *Tapovana*. He writes: "A most wonderful thing that we notice in India is, that here the forest, not the town, is the fountain-head of all its civilisation. Wherever in India its earliest and most wonderful manifestations are noticed, we find that here men have not come into so close contact as to be rolled or pushed into a compact body, or mass, or whole. Here, trees and plants, rivers and lakes, had an ample opportunity to live in close relationship with men. In these forests, though there was human society, there was enough of open space, or aloofness; there was no jostling. Still, this aloofness did not produce an inertness in the Indian mind; on the other hand, it rendered it all the brighter. It is the forest that has nurtured the two great ancient ages of India, the Vedic and the Buddhistic. Not only the Vedic Ṛṣis, but Lord Buddha also preached in many woods of India. The Royal Palace had no room for him, it was the forest that took him into its lap. The current of civilisation that flowed from the forest inundated the whole of India".[2]

---

1 Tāranāth says that Pandit Sākyaśrī went to Odevisa and thence to Tibet.

2 I do not know whether the late Mr. Charles Russell and Mr. V. H. Jackson had this in view when in the *Patna University Report* they

Such was also the Vikramśilā University and all the other ancient Indian Universities. As I have said already that although there was close connection between the Brāhmanical and the Buddhist methods of teaching, there was one main difference between the Brāhmanic and the Buddhist education, *viz.*, that the latter was not based on Vedic study and its teachers were not invariably Brāhmanas. Further, Buddhistic education was open to one and all, and not merely to the three "twice-born" castes. All castes were equally admissible to the Buddhistic community. Defects there were in both the system, but "meaningless and trivial as many of these regulations seem to us, they were no doubt regarded as of great value by those who used them in those far-off days. They must have been intended to emphasize the great solemnity of the work in which pupil and teacher were engaged, and to impress upon the pupil the mysterious sacredness which was supposed to characterise the knowledge which was being passed on to him by his teacher."[2] This may sound as a mere ideal to us now.

But we cannot forget that everywhere the same ideal was preached in Ancient India: "Say what is true; do thy duty; do not swerve from the truth; do not swerve from duty; do not neglect greatness; do not neglect what is useful. Whatever is given should be given with faith, not without faith, with joy, with modesty, with fear and with kindness. If there should be any doubt in thy mind with regard to any sacred act or with regard to conduct, conduct thyself as a Brahmana"[1]. As one who has been closely

observed: "In our opinion the ideally best site would be in some healthy situation removed from the influence of any large town and where could be carried on under favourable climatic conditions throughout the whole academic year."

2 Keays, *Ancient Indian Education*, p. 37.

1 *Taitt. Upanişada*, 1, 4, 3.

associated and, may I add, intimately also, with the students of Magadha for over a decade, I do not think I can hold up before them a better ideal than what was placed by Chānakya before the princes at Pātaliputra with whose teaching he was entrusted and to whom he observed : "The King is honoured only in his own kingdom, the learned are honoured throughout the world". The erudite *Āchāryyas* of Magadha were honoured throughout the then civilised world for their learning, —and who does not even now revere Mahāvīra and Buddha ?—and I can fervently hope that with such glorious ideals before them, our students should not be wanting in example. Let them remember what manner of men their forefathers were, and if they have before them such glorious ideals of which, I hope, I have been able to give them some idea, I will consider myself more than amply rewarded for delivering these lectures on the glories of Magadha, their and our own Mother land.

The poet has truly observed :—

"Breathes there the man with soul so dead,
Who never to himself hath said,
This is my own my native land !"

Sir Sultan Ahmad, Vice-chancellor of the University, in concluding the course of Lectures observed :

"Gentlemen, as this is the last of a series of very interesting lectures delivered by Professor Samaddar as our University Reader, I would be failing in my duty if I did not convey him our hearfelt thanks for the same.

Professor Samaddar has been in this Province for a number of years and his work as a research scholar and a Professor of History, his keen interest in Archæology and Economics, his connection with all the healthy public activities of the students here, his work on the Senate and his particular interest in the students who come in close contact with him are wellknown. The Calcutta University paid him, and incidentally to this University, a great compliment when they invited him to give a series of lectures which were ultimately published by them. I have seen these lectures and I can assure you that they fully maintain the high standard of scholarship which is now attributed to his name. Professor Samaddar has given us six most interesting and instructive lectures which when published will, I have no doubt, be a great contribution to the ancient history of Magadha. The masterly manner in which he has dealt with his subject and the scientific study which these erudite lectures display are only surpassed by the lucidity of expression and accuracy of facts. On some matters he has differed from well-known scholars like my friend Mr. Jayaswal and Professor Bhandarkar and he has given his reasons for taking a different view. Whether he is right or whether those from whom he has differed are correct, is a matter on which an expression of opinion will be hazardous, nor indeed do I consider myself fully competent to express my views. The lectures, once published, will be open to discussion and criticism. But whatever the result of that discussion may be, I have no doubt even those from whom he has differed will acknowledge that Professor Samaddar has been a worthy opponent. *I thank him, as the Vice-chancellor of the University, for having accepted the readership without* any honorarium; I thank him personally as well as on your behalf for the extremely learned lectures, as I feel that these have materially contributed to the stock of our knowledge of the ancient history of the province."

LIST OF PLATES

For accounts relating to the excavations at Nālandā, see *Annual Report of the Archeological Survey of India*, Eastern Circle, 1915-1916 and *Archaeological Survey Reports* of subsequent years.

22. P. 131. *Hilsā Statue* : See *J. B. & O. R. S.*, X. 37. (By courtesy of the Bihar & Orissa Research Society).

23. P. 136. *The Temple at Buddha Gaya* (after repairs): See Cunningham and Mitra.

24. P. 136. *The Buddha Gaya Temple* (before repairs). See ante.

25 & 26. P. 153. *Parts of frieze at Vikramaśilā* : (Reproduced for the first time).

INDEX

PAGES

PAGES